広島被爆地図　areas of Hiroshima affected by

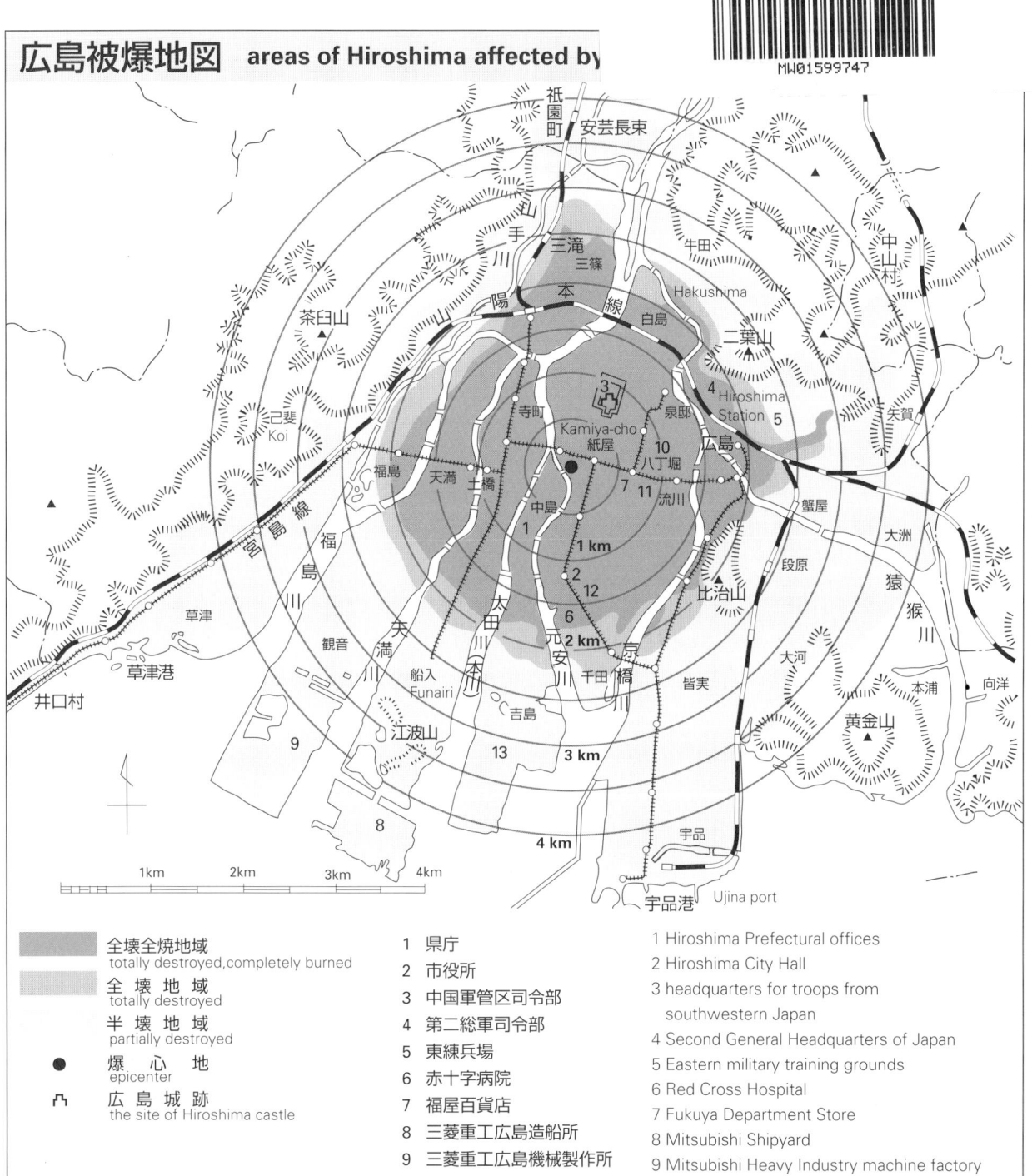

凡例 / Legend

	全壊全焼地域 totally destroyed, completely burned
	全壊地域 totally destroyed
	半壊地域 partially destroyed
●	爆心地 epicenter
卍	広島城跡 the site of Hiroshima castle

1　県庁 — 1 Hiroshima Prefectural offices
2　市役所 — 2 Hiroshima City Hall
3　中国軍管区司令部 — 3 headquarters for troops from southwestern Japan
4　第二総軍司令部 — 4 Second General Headquarters of Japan
5　東練兵場 — 5 Eastern military training grounds
6　赤十字病院 — 6 Red Cross Hospital
7　福屋百貨店 — 7 Fukuya Department Store
8　三菱重工広島造船所 — 8 Mitsubishi Shipyard
9　三菱重工広島機械製作所 — 9 Mitsubishi Heavy Industry machine factory
10　中央放送局 — 10 Chuo Broadcasting Services
11　中国新聞社 — 11 The Chugoku Shimbun Newspaper offices
12　広島文理科大学 — 12 Hiroshima University
13　陸軍飛行場 — 13 Army airport

※施設の名称は当時のもの。

はじめに

　15年間にわたるアジア・太平洋戦争が、日本の敗戦で終結してから今日までの60年間、日本は平和を保持してきた。それは他国の人を戦争によって殺害したことは一度もないということであった。多数の人々による不戦の願いと、それを支える「日本国憲法」の存在こそが平和を維持する原動力であった。

　敗戦を迎える直前に、原子爆弾がアメリカによって広島・長崎に投下された。その炸裂と爆風によって二つの都市は壊滅し、20万を超える市民が犠牲となった。そして撒き散らされた放射能によって、さらに多くの人が「緩慢なる死」を余儀なくされ、今も死と向き合っている。

　戦後60年──その歴史の原点に、この被爆体験がある。それは平和の原点であると同時に、人類が直面している「核時代」の原点でもある。

　原点を風化させてはならない。事あるごとに原点に立ち返り、私たち自身のありようや日本・世界の未来を考えねばならないと強く思う。

　「ノーモア　ヒロシマ・ナガサキ」──本書は、そんな願いをもとに編まれ、刊行される。

Preface

　Since its defeat after fifteen years of war in Asia and the Pacific, Japan has preserved the peace. For sixty years now Japan has not once killed a foreign national through an act of war. This preservation of the peace is driven by both a widespread aversion to war and a document that supports that aversion: the Constitution of Japan.

　On the eve of Japan's defeat, the United States dropped atomic bombs on the cities of Hiroshima and Nagasaki. The explosions turned the two cities to ruins and killed over 200,000 people. The radiation that washed over the cities condemned many others to a "lingering death," an affliction that torments some even today.

　Japan's sixty years of postwar history are rooted in its experience of the atomic bombings. That event defined its peace; that event marks the advent of the nuclear age facing humankind today.

　This point of origin must not be forgotten. We sincerely believe that it is the point to which we must return at all critical junctures in order to consider once again who we are and what we want for the future of both Japan and the world.

　We have therefore edited and published this book in hopes that there will be "No More Hiroshima, Nagasaki."

　1945年8月6日午前8時15分、広島にウラニウム原子爆弾が炸裂。そのエネルギーはTNT1トン火薬爆弾の1万2,500倍であったとされる。写真はその瞬間からおよそ1時間後、作戦に参加したB29爆撃機3機のうちの1機が撮影したキノコ雲。真夏の太陽に不気味に光る巨大なキノコ雲の下に、ヒロシマの悲惨な「うめき」が聞こえる。（撮影／米軍　提供／広島平和記念資料館）

On 6 August 1945, at 8:15 a.m., a uranium-type atomic bomb exploded over Hiroshima, releasing 12,500 times more energy than one ton of TNT. This photograph, taken from one of the three B29 bombers participating in the mission, captures the mushroom cloud approximately one hour after detonation. Beneath this gigantic mushroom cloud glinting sickeningly in the bright summer sunlight, the city of Hiroshima wailed in agony. (Photo by the U.S.Army; provided courtesy of Hiroshima Peace Memorial Museum.)

No More Hiroshima, Nagasaki

原爆写真　ノーモア ヒロシマ・ナガサキ

黒古一夫　清水博義　編

日本図書センター

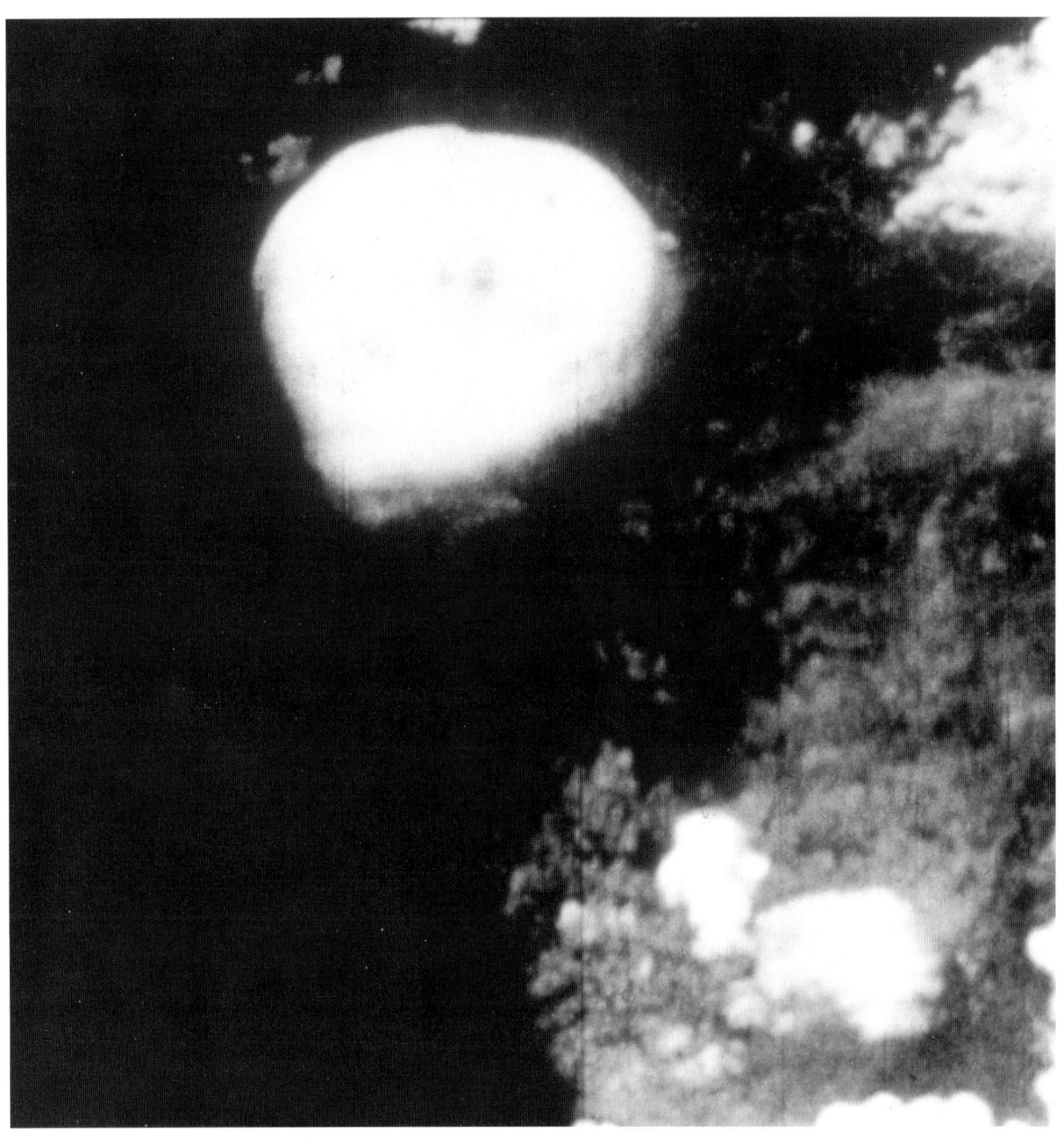

1945年8月9日午前11時2分、長崎にプルトニウム原子爆弾が投下された。写真は炸裂の瞬間。そのエネルギーはTNT1トン火薬爆弾のおよそ2万2,000倍。発生したエネルギーの約35%が熱線、50%が爆風、15%が放射線エネルギーであったと推定されている。（撮影／米軍　提供／平和博物館を創る会＝日本の市民運動により1980年に入手）

On 9 August 1945, at 11:02 a.m., a plutonium-type atomic bomb was dropped on Nagasaki. This photo captures the moment of detonation, which released 22,000 times more energy than a ton of TNT. Studies estimate that 35% of the energy was released as heat rays, 50% as blast, and 15% as radiation.(Photo by the U.S. Army; provided courtesy of Association to Establish the Japan Peace Museum through the assistance of grass-roots movements in Japan, 1980.)

目次

Edited by Kuroko Kazuo & Shimizu Hiroyoshi
English translation by James Dorsey
Book design, layout by Kobayashi Kenzo (Nikori Design).

First Edition, 2005.
Published by Nihon Tosho Center CO., LTD.
3-8-2, Otsuka, Bunkyo-ku, Tokyo
Copyright 2005 by Nihon Tosho Center CO., LTD; all rights reserved.
Printed in Japan.
ISBN 4-8205-1940-9

Table of Contents

序（『原爆詩集』）　　峠　三吉

ちちをかえせ　ははをかえせ
としよりをかえせ
こどもをかえせ

わたしをかえせ　わたしにつながる
にんげんをかえせ

にんげんの　にんげんのよのあるかぎり
くずれぬへいわを
へいわをかえせ

"Preface" to Songs of Hiroshima　　　　**Toge Sankichi**

Give back our fathers, give back our mothers.
Give back our elderly.
Give back our children.

Give me back myself.
Give back those who have meant something to me.

A human peace, a peace that lasts
As long as this world is to be a human world.
Give back the peace.

とうげ・さんきち（1917〜1953）広島県生まれ。爆心地より3kmの自宅で被爆。叙情詩人でクリスチャンだった峠は、戦後、政治運動に積極的に参加する。反戦・反原爆の代表的詩人。詩集に『原爆詩集』『峠三吉作品集』（全2巻）などがある。

Toge Sankichi (1917~1953). Born in Hiroshima, Toge was in his home 3 kilometers from the epicenter when the bomb was dropped. Already a poet and Christian, after the war Toge became an energetic political activist as well. A representative anti-war, anti-nuclear poet, his works include Songs of Hiroshima and Poems by Toge Sankichi (2 volumes).

広
HIROSHIMA
島

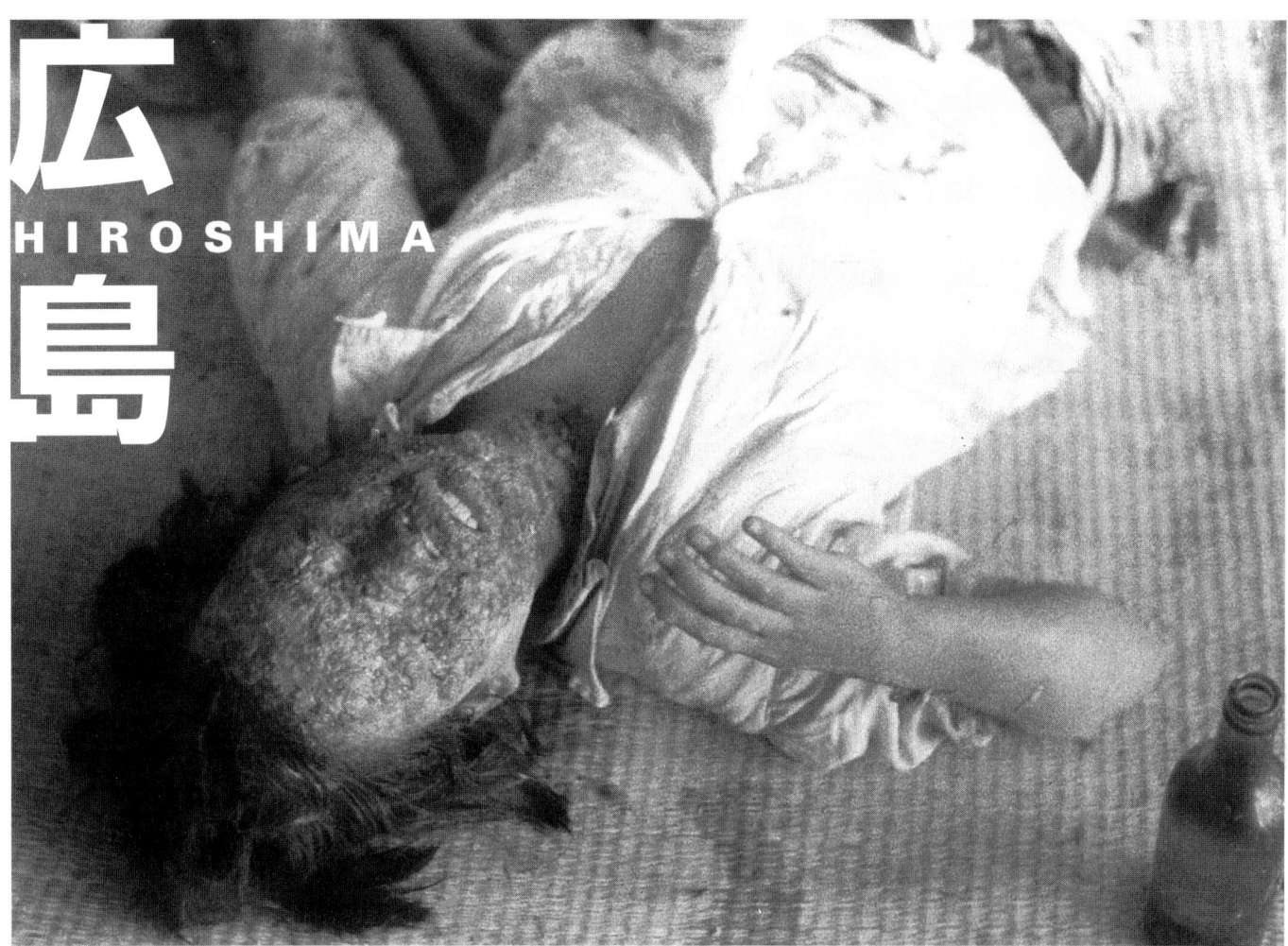

　戦後、日本を占領した連合軍（アメリカ軍中心）は、原爆報道を厳しく制限した。日本国民が被爆の悲惨を初めて知ったのは、被爆から7年後、1952年8月6日号の「アサヒグラフ」によってであった。被爆直後に朝日新聞のカメラマンが撮影したフィルムは、ずっと編集長のデスクに眠っていた。同誌の発売をきっかけに、被爆の実相を伝える記録や詩歌・写真などが報道・出版されるようになった。

　　In the postwar period the Allied occupation forces (with U.S. troops at the core) strictly suppressed information pertaining to the atomic bombings. Though photographers for the Asahi Shimbun Newspaper had chronicled the days immediately following the bombings, their film had remained untouched on the desks of their editors, and it was only a full seven years later, in the 6 August 1952 edition of the magazine *Asahi Graph*, that the people of Japan first learned of the horrors of the atomic bombings. This article in the *Asahi Graph* paved the way for further media coverage and the publication of photographs, poetry, and detailed information revealing the truth about the atomic bombs.

顔面に熱傷を負った動員学徒の女学生
広島赤十字病院に運び込まれたものの、手当てもされず、ゴザの上で「水！水！」とあえぎながら、傍らに置かれた水を飲む気力もなく、やがて息を引き取っていった。（撮影／被爆4日目・宮武甫　提供／朝日新聞社）

Facial burns suffered by a mobilized female student. Though carried to the Hiroshima Red Cross Hospital, she received no treatment. She moaned for water as she lay on a mat, but was without the strength to drink from the bottle that had been set beside her. Before long she stopped breathing. (Photo by Miyatake Hajime, provided courtesy of the Asahi Shimbun Newspaper, three days after bombing.)

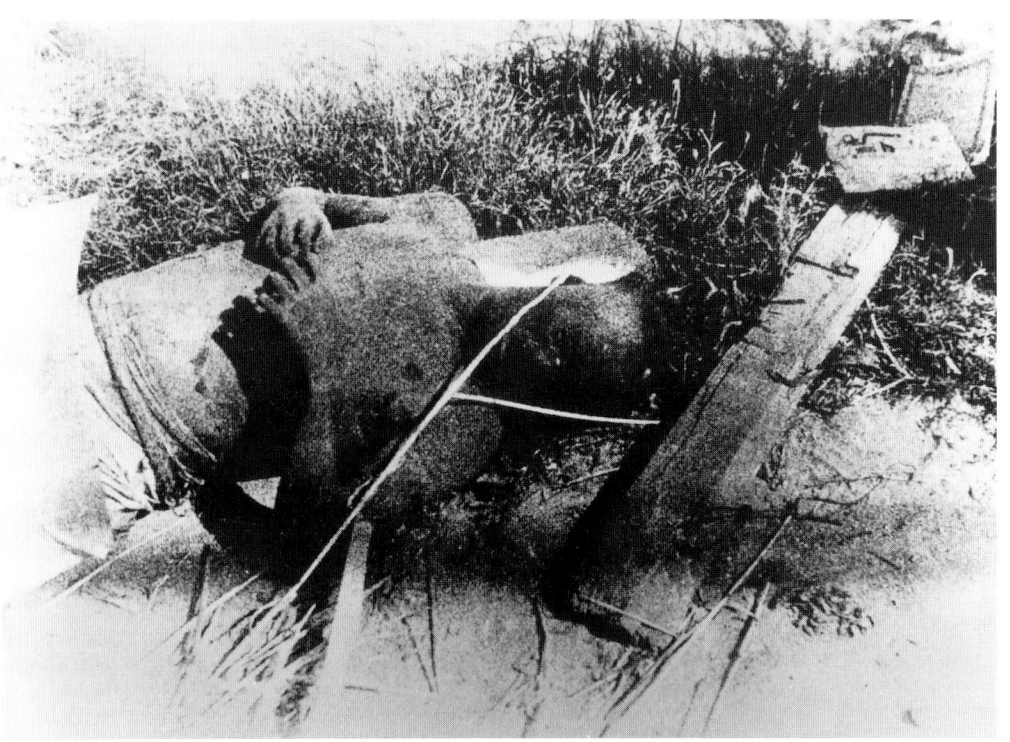

熱線と爆風圧を受けた兵士の遺体　爆心地から北東700〜800mにある西練兵場。誰かが白い布を顔にかぶせていた。この辺りは中国軍管区司令部はじめ軍の諸部隊が集中していたが、すべて壊滅し、死の広場と化した。（撮影／被爆4日目・中田佐都男　提供／広島平和記念資料館）

Corpse of a soldier killed by the heat rays and the blast. Someone had placed a white cloth over the face of this victim, found at the western military training grounds. The area housed a high concentration of military units, including the command personnel for all troops from southwestern Japan. Everything was destroyed and the area was strewn with the dead. (Photo by Nakata Satsuo, provided courtesy of Hiroshima Peace Memorial Museum, three days after the bombing.)

集められる遺体　死傷をまぬがれた人たちは直ちに市内に駆けつけ、救護隊に協力した。至る所に折り重なって倒れる遺体を河原や広場に集め、荼毘（だび）に付した。幽気をはらんだ煙が何日にもわたって市中を包んだ。（撮影／宮武甫　提供／朝日新聞社）

Gathering the corpses. Those who had escaped death and injury poured quickly into the city to aid in the rescue efforts. They collected the corpses lying tangled in heaps in every corner of the city and carried them to the riverside or neighborhood squares, where they cremated the bodies. For days on end the city was enveloped in the smoke carrying the tortured souls of the dead. (Photo by Miyatake Hajime, provided courtesy of the Asahi Shimbun Newspaper.)

ヒロシマの惨禍

The Tragedy of Hiroshima

1945（昭和20）年８月６日午前８時15分、西日本最大の軍事都市広島に投下された世界で最初の核兵器＝原子爆弾（通称「リトルボーイ」長さ３ｍ、直径0.7ｍ、重さ４ｔ）は、一瞬にして30万人余りの人口を抱えた都市の90％を壊滅させ、約14万人の死者（1945年末までの集計）とほぼ同数の「被爆者」を生み出した。

市の中心部580ｍの上空で摂氏100万度、数十万気圧の火球となり強力な熱線と放射線、そして爆風を短時間に四方へ放射したこの原爆は、マンハッタン計画＝原爆開発計画を推進した人びとの予想をはるかに超える破壊力と殺傷力を持つものであった。

阿鼻叫喚の中、逃げまどう人びと。火炎にまかれ、あるいは爆風によって倒壊した建物の下敷きになって助けを求める人びと。運良く惨劇から逃れたとしても身体を貫いた放射能によって体内を破壊され、幾日も生きられなかった人びと。これらの人びとの多くが、女性や子ども、老人といった非戦闘員＝無辜の民であった。戦争の結果とはいえ、これほどの破壊と殺戮が許されるのか。広島市にもたらされた「未曾有の破壊・殺戮」は、これまでの人類が経験したどの戦争でも起こらなかったことであり、この地上に出現した「地獄」といわれるのも故なきことではなかったのである。

ヒロシマが「地獄」であった理由は、単にそれが未だかつて人類が経験したことのない大規模な破壊や殺戮だったからだけではない。原爆病＝放射能障害の発病を恐れ、生きながら常に「死」を意識せざるを得ない「ヒバクシャ」を大量に生じさせたことも、この大量破壊兵器＝原爆が通常兵器と決定的に異なっていたことであった。

ヒロシマは、私たち人類とそれを育む地球に「終わり」があることを告げた。「ノーモア・ヒロシマ」は、私たち人類の悲願である。ヒロシマを、忘れてはならない。

On 6 August 1945, at 8:15 a.m., the world's first nuclear weapon, an atomic bomb, was dropped on western Japan's largest militarized city, Hiroshima. Nicknamed "Little Boy," the bomb was 3 meters in length, 0.7 meters in diameter, and it weighed 4 tons. In an instant 90% of this city, with a population of 300,000, was destroyed. According to calculations made at the end of 1945, 140,000 individuals had died and there was an almost equal number of "hibakusha," people exposed to the bomb's radiation.

From its epicenter 580 meters above the center of the city, the atomic bomb produced a fireball reaching temperatures of over a million degrees celsius and generated a blast measuring several hundred thousand atmospheres of pressure. The bomb also released an intense barrage of heat rays and radiation that washed over the city. In terms of its capability to destroy property and inflict injury, the weapon far exceeded even the expectations of those involved in the Manhattan Project, the enterprise that had developed the atomic bomb.

Some residents of the city were left disoriented and frantically seeking an escape from the sea of fire. Others were trapped by the flames or pinned beneath buildings toppled by the blast. These people could do nothing but cry for help. Others were fortunate enough to have survived the explosion, but the radiation had ravaged their internal organs and they were to die in a matter of days. Many of these people were innocent noncombatants-- women, children, and the elderly. Surely even those resigned to idea that casualties are a cruel fact of war must balk at the scale of this carnage and destruction. It was truly unprecedented, without parallel in any war waged by humankind. It is with good reason that Hiroshima has been called a "hell on earth."

It is not only the scope of the devastation that warrants the label of a "hell on earth." Equally important is a second characteristic that distinguishes the atomic bomb as a weapon of mass destruction from conventional weapons: its creation of "hibakusha," the victims of the bomb's radiation. In constant fear of an onset of radiation sickness (the atomic bomb disease), the "hibakusha" live always in the shadow of death.

Hiroshima has taught us that for both humankind and the earth that nurtures it, there is such a thing as an "end." As members of the human race we share a desperate hope: "No more Hiroshima." We must not forget.

人間を返せ
"原爆砂漠"のなかで…

Give back the people!
Scenes from an atomic wasteland.

警官派出所前の惨状　被爆当日の午前11時頃撮られた写真。臨時の避難所となった派出所で、集まってくる被爆者に警察官が食用油をぬって手当てした。被爆者のなかには、建物疎開にたずさわっていた広島女子商業学校、県立第一中学校の生徒が多くいた。
　当時、中国新聞社の写真部員だった松重さんは「あまりのむごたらしさ、恐ろしさに被爆者を正面から撮影することができなかった」と語っている。（撮影／松重美人　所蔵／中国新聞社　提供／広島平和記念資料館）

Misery in front of the police box.
The photo was taken at approximately 11 a.m. on the morning of the bombing. This neighborhood police box had become a makeshift evacuation center, and the policemen provided first-aid by rubbing cooking oil on the burns of the victims who gathered there. This group included many students from Hiroshima Girls' Commercial School and the First Prefectural Middle School. They had been in the city to create firebreaks by dismantling buildings.
Matsushige Yoshito, photographer for the Chugoku Shimbun Newspaper at the time, stated: "it was so shocking and horrific that I could not photograph these atomic bomb victims from the front." (Photo by Matsushige Yoshito, owned by the Chugoku Shimbun Newspaper, provided courtesy of Hiroshima Peace Memorial Museum.)

荒野と化した広島市　上は護国神社付近から神社の鳥居、右に産業奨励館（原爆ドーム）がむき出して望めた。下は中国新聞社の煙突に上って撮った南西のデルタ。右の山に瓦礫となった己斐町。いずれも、数カットをつないで360度のパノラマ写真にした、その一部。

　被爆1か月後、撮影者の林さんは原子爆弾学術調査団のカメラマンとして広島・長崎に入った。「これがただ一発の爆弾で破壊された街なのか──。どうしても受け入れることができない

まま、私は爆心地に立ちつくしていた。…どの建物の亀裂跡も、荼毘に付されたまま放置された遺骨も、戦争を否定する絶叫のように私には聞こえた」（撮影／林重男　提供／広島平和記念資料館）

The barren plain that was once Hiroshima. The photo at the top of the page shows the *torii* gate and area surrounding the Gokoku Shrine; to the right is the skeleton of the Hiroshima Prefectural Industrial Promotion Hall (now known as the Atomic Bomb Dome). The photo directly above was taken from atop the chimney of the Chugoku Shimbun Newspaper office building and shows the delta to the southwest. Against the mountain to the right is Koimachi, reduced to rubble. Both are excerpted from a multiple frame, 360° panoramic.

A month after the bombings, Hayashi Shigeo visited Hiroshima and Nagasaki as a photographer for the Atomic Bomb Research Team. "I stood dumbfounded at ground zero, unable to accept the fact that this city had been decimated by a single bomb. . . . The fractures in the building walls, the abandoned bones of cremated victims--all of it struck me as a scream denouncing war." (Photo by Hayashi Shigeo, provided courtesy of Hiroshima Peace Memorial Museum.)

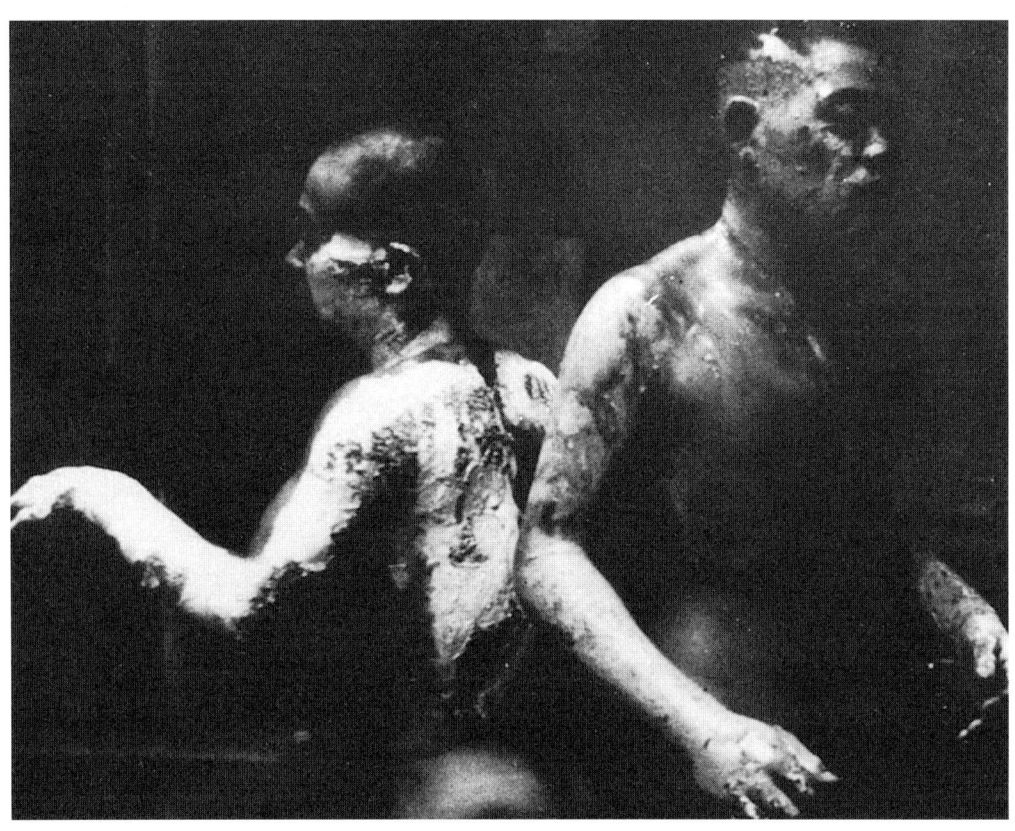

全身焼けただれた二人　似島臨時救護所で。似島は広島市から4km南に位置し、海外から帰国する兵士たち全員を検査する検疫所があった。被爆後直ちに臨時の救護所がもうけられ、被爆者が殺到したが、その多くは死亡した。（撮影者不詳）

Two victims with full-body burns. Photo taken at the provisional first-aid station at Ninoshima island. Located 4 kilometers south of Hiroshima, Ninoshima was home to the quarantine base for all repatriated military men. A makeshift first-aid station was set up there in the immediate wake of the bombing, but was soon flooded with "*hibakusha*," the majority of whom died. (Photographer unknown.)

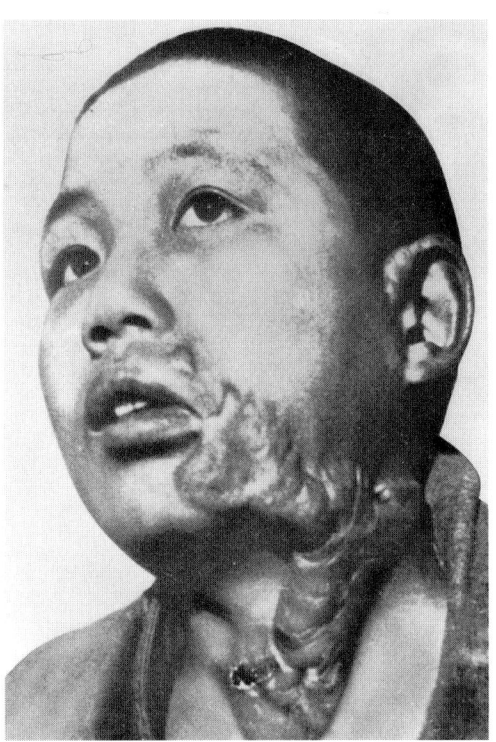 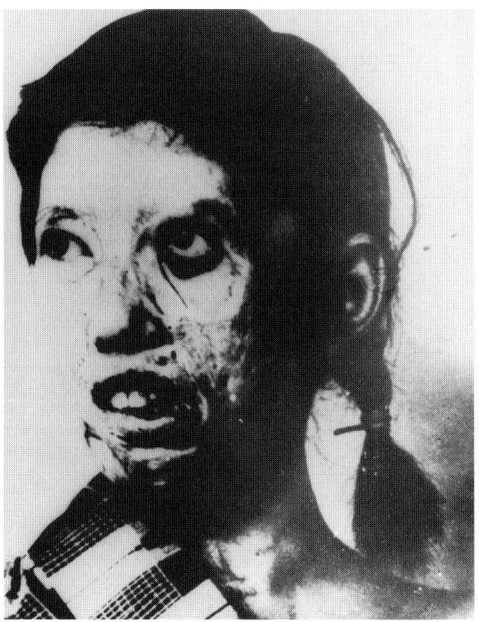

（左）ケロイドの男性　似島臨時救護所で。（撮影者不詳）
（右）ケロイドの女性　広島赤十字病院で。放射線科技手だった黒石さんは、手術を施した被爆者を医学的資料として撮影した。「治療の甲斐なく、数日を待たずして次々と亡くなっていかれた。思わず合掌する日々だった」（撮影／黒石勝）

left: Man suffering from keloids. Photo taken at the Ninoshima first-aid station. (Photographer unknown.)
right: Woman suffering from keloids. Photo taken at Hiroshima Red Cross Hospital by Kuroishi Masaru, an x-ray technician who photographed surgery patients in order to medically document their progress. "The treatments proved ineffective, and within a matter of days, one right after the other, the patients died," he said. "I often found myself putting my hands together in prayer." (Photo by Kuroishi Masaru.)

熱傷を負った兵士　似島臨時救護所で。腹巻が巻かれていた腰の皮膚だけが負傷をまぬがれた。（撮影／被爆翌日・尾糠政美）

Soldier with burn wounds.
Photo taken at the Ninoshima first-aid center. Only the skin around his waist, which had been wrapped with a stomach warmer, escaped the burns. (Photo by Onuka Masami, the day after the bombing.)

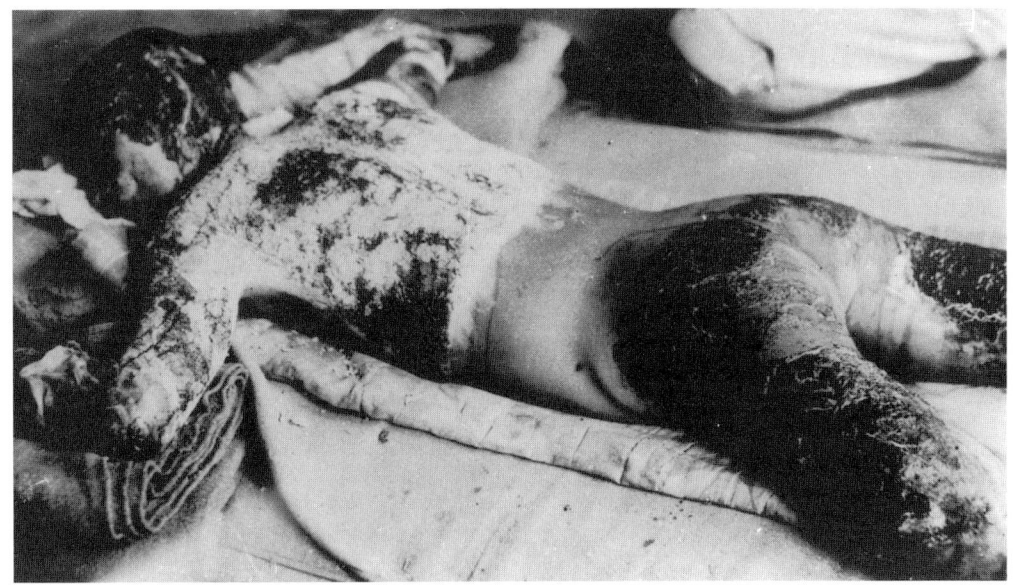

防空壕から掘り出された白骨死体　被爆から5年後の1950年、現在、広島市民球場がある基町の地下2mから発掘された。防空壕のなかで蒸し焼きになり、骨だけが残ったものだろう。（撮影／佐々木雄一郎）

Skeleton excavated from an air-raid shelter. This victim's remains were uncovered from a depth of 2 meters in 1950, five years after the bombing. The site was Motomachi, the area where the Hiroshima Municipal Baseball Field stands today. It is believed the victim was literally "baked" in the dugout, leaving only his skeleton. (Photo by Sasaki Yuichiro.)

11

被爆前の広島産業奨励館　チェコの建築家ヤン・レツルが、川辺に映える斬新な建物をと設計した。（撮影者不詳）

The Hiroshima Prefectural Industrial Promotion Hall before the bombing. Czech architect Jan Letzel's novel design for this building positioned it so that it would be reflected in the water of the river. (Photographer unknown.)

被爆前の広島城
（撮影者不詳）

被爆後の広島産業奨励館（現・原爆ドーム）爆心地より150m。被爆直後、もっとも早く撮られたとされる写真。1996年、原爆ドームは世界遺産に登録された。（撮影／松重美人　所蔵／中国新聞社 提供／広島平和記念資料館）

The Hiroshima Prefectural Industrial Promotion Hall (The A-Bomb Dome) after the bombing. This building, located 150 meters from the epicenter, was registered on the UNESCO World Heritage List in 1996. (Photo by Matsushige Yoshito, owned by the Chugoku Shimbun Newspaper, provided courtesy of Hiroshima Peace Memorial Museum.)

原爆で吹き飛んだ広島城の跡
（撮影／松重美人　所蔵／中国新聞社　提供／広島平和記念資料館）

生から死へ、一瞬の崩壊

　広島は太田川下流のデルタを中心に開け、南は瀬戸内海に面した「水の都」として発展した。市を流れる6本の川が、橋の多い独特な景観を生み出していた。北は重なる山並みが幾重にも続き、街はその間を縫うように広がっていた。また、明治から昭和にかけての相次ぐ戦争のなかで、広島は中国大陸進出への足場となり、軍の主要基地としての性格も強めていった。

　1945年初頭から始まる日本列島へのアメリカ軍の大空襲は、東京はじめ大阪・名古屋・横浜・神戸など主要都市のほとんどを焼き尽くしたが、広島は京都・奈良・長崎・新潟・小倉など、数少ない無傷の都市の一つとして残ってい

た。原爆の威力を誇示するには無傷の都市が必要だった。

　8月6日朝、戦時下とはいえ、人びとのいつもの日常が始まろうとしていた。次の瞬間に起こる「地獄図」を誰一人想像することもなく……。

　軍都とはいえ、歴史ある美しい街の、熱線と爆風による一瞬の崩壊であった。

Hiroshima Castle before the bomb.
(Photographer unknown.)

被爆前の繁華街・広島本通り
（撮影者不詳）

The Hondori shopping arcade in Hiroshima's shopping district before the bombing.
(Photographer unknown.)

Hiroshima Castle after the bomb, the blast leaving only the foundation.
(Photo by Matsushige Yoshito, owned by the Chugoku Shimbun Newspaper, provided courtesy of Hiroshima Peace Memorial Museum.)

被爆直後の広島本通り
（撮影者不詳）

The Hondori shopping arcade immediately after the bombing.
(Photographer unknown.)

From Life to Death: Instantaneous Destruction

Started on the delta of the lower branches of the Ota River and facing the Inland Sea to the south, Hiroshima has always been a city defined by its waters, and its striking landscape is distinguished by the many bridges spanning the six rivers that flow through it. A number of mountain ridges stretch out to the north of the city, and the newer neighborhoods thread their way between them. Beginning in 1894, Hiroshima served as a jump-off point for Japan's numerous military campaigns on the Asian continent, and its reputation as an important military center grew.

Early 1945 saw the start of intensive U.S. air raids over the islands of Japan. Before long the major metropolitan areas of Tokyo, Osaka, Yokohama, Nagoya and Kobe had all been turned to ruins. Hiroshima, however, like Kyoto, Nara, Nagasaki, Niigata, and Kokura, was one of the few select cities that remained unscathed. As such it was a perfect showpiece for the power of the atomic bomb.

Though the country was at war, 6 August started much like any other day for the people of Hiroshima. Not one of them could possibly have imagined that the world around them would soon resemble a "hell screen," one of the horrifying Buddhist paintings depicting the fate of the damned. The city was instantaneously destroyed by the blast and the heat rays. Gone was a militarized city--and with it went a beautiful metropolis with its own distinguished history.

原子爆弾は市のほぼ中心、580ｍの上空で強烈な閃光を放ち炸裂、灼熱の火球は一瞬のうちに直径280ｍの大きさにふくれあがった。火球の中心温度は摂氏100万度を超え、爆心地周辺の地上温度は3,000～4,000度にも達した。

炸裂と同時に超高熱の熱線と放射能が放たれ、超音速で進む衝撃波と次いで秒速700ｍにも及ぶ大爆風が全市を襲った。被害は広島市の全域に及び、建物の約90％が焼失、あるいは倒壊した。本書の冒頭に掲載した「広島被爆地図」を参照してほしい。

The atomic bomb exploded 580 meters above the center of city, releasing an intense flash of light and a mighty fireball that instantly expanded to 280 meters in diameter. Temperatures at the center of the fireball reached over a million degrees celsius; temperatures on the ground beneath the epicenter reached 3,000 to 4,000 degrees.

Heat rays and radioactivity were released, and a shockwave travelling at supersonic speeds swept over the city. Immediately following was a blast of air reaching speeds of up to 700 meters per second. Damage was done all over the city, with 90% of the buildings either burned or knocked over by the blast. Please refer to the "Hiroshima Atomic Bomb Map" included at the front of this volume.

爆心地から原爆ドームを望む
（撮影／1945年10月・佐々木雄一郎）

View of the Atomic Bomb Dome from ground zero. (Photo by Sasaki Yuichiro, October 1945.)

倒壊した鉄筋コンクリート建築　大手町3丁目、広島ガス本社。（撮影／1945年秋・川本俊雄　提供／広島平和記念資料館）

アメ細工のように曲がりくねった鉄骨　爆心地から840m、旧中国新聞社裏にあった小田政倉庫の鉄骨。（撮影／1946年4月・空博行　提供／広島平和記念資料館）

被爆した市電　紙屋町交差点から東へ270mで被爆。一人の生存者を除き全員が死亡したという。（撮影／1945年9月・川原四儀　提供／広島平和記念資料館）

Left: **Collapsed building of reinforced concrete.** The Hiroshima Gas Co., Ohtemachi 3 chome. (Photo by Kawamoto Toshio, provided courtesy of Hiroshima Peace Memorial Museum, Autumn 1945.)

Lower left: **Iron framework twisted like a pretzel.** The Oda masa Warehouse behind the old Chugoku Shimbun Newspaper office building, 840 meters from ground zero. (Photo by Sora Hiroyuki, provided courtesy of Hiroshima Peace Memorial Museum, April 1946.)

Lower right: **Streetcar exposed to the blast.** It was located 270 meters east of the Kamiya-cho intersection at the time of the bombing. All but one passenger died. (Photo by Kawahara Yotsugi, provided courtesy of Hiroshima Peace Memorial Museum, September 1945.)

熱線の恐怖

The Horror of the Heat Rays

　熱線は、人間にケロイドの刻印を焼き付け、建物を燃やし尽くしただけではない。その恐怖は、石段や壁に残る人影、路面に焼き付く欄干の影、ガスタンクに残るハンドルの影、さまざまな植物などにも現われていた。

　The heat rays left keloids on those exposed and incinerated whole buildings. Their horrific force also burned human silhouettes onto stone stairways, outlines of railings onto roadways, and the shadows of levers onto tanks holding natural gas. Plant life of every sort, too, was scorched.

（左）石段に焼き付けられた人影　紙屋町1丁目の住友銀行入口に残った人の影。爆心地から東へ250mの地点。遺体を収容した人の証言で、当日の朝、銀行の開店を待って石段に腰掛けていた女性の影だと推定されている。この石段は、後に広島平和記念資料館に収められ、保存されている。（撮影／1946年頃・松重美人　所蔵／中国新聞社　提供／広島平和記念資料館）

A human silhouette burned into a stone staircase. This photo shows a human silhouette left on the stone entrance to the Sumitomo Bank in Kamiya-cho, 1-chome, located 250 meters to the east of ground zero. Based on the testimony of the person who retrieved the body, the shadow was cast by a woman sitting on the steps as she waited for the bank to open on the morning of the bombing. This stone staircase is now housed and preserved in the Hiroshima Peace Memorial Museum. (Photo by Matsushige Yoshito, owned by the Chugoku Shimbun Newspaper, provided courtesy of Hiroshima Peace Memorial Museum, 1946.)

（右）焼けただれたダイダイの実　爆心地より3km、己斐町で。付近の茶臼山は一帯に焼け焦げていた。（撮影／菊池俊吉）

Scorched tangerine. This photo was taken in Koimachi, 3 kilometers from ground zero. Nearby Mt. Chausu was completely charred. (Photo by Kikuchi Shunkichi .)

臨時救護所

Provisional First-Aid Stations

銀行であれ、学校・デパートであれ、かろうじて外壁をとどめた建物は、臨時の救護施設・病院となった。川辺や広場には、大小のテントも張られた。市内53か所で医師や看護婦が献身的な治療にあたったが、彼らもまた被爆者であり、医薬品も絶対的に不足していた。

収容された被爆者は11月までに10万人を超え、外来患者は20万人以上。市内を逃れ、郡部に避難場所を求めた人は、およそ15万人だったとされる。かろうじて救護所に運ばれ、たどりついた人々も、日を追って息を引き取っていった。

Banks, schools, department stores--any building with four walls standing was turned into a temporary first-aid station or clinic. Tents, both large and small, were also pitched along the river and in city plazas to serve the same purpose. Doctors and nurses dedicated themselves to treating casualties in 53 locations throughout the city, but they, too, were victims of the bomb and they faced a crushing shortage of medical supplies.

Over 100,000 atomic-bomb casualties were housed in these facilities through the end of November, with outpatients numbering over twice that. Approximately 150,000 others fled the city entirely, seeking help in the surrounding areas. Many of those who stumbled into these first aid stations or arrived on stretchers died soon after.

救護所であえぐ人々 爆心地より1,2km、太田川のほとりに設置された広島第二陸軍病院の大テントの被爆者。（撮影／1945年8月9日・陸軍船舶司令部写真部・川原四儀 提供／広島平和記念資料館）

People seeking assistance at a first-aid station. These photos show atomic bomb victims at the big tent set up by the Second Hiroshima Army Hospital on the banks of the Ota River, 1,2kirometers from ground zero. (Photo by Kawahara Yotsugi of the Army Marine Command Photography Squad, provided courtesy of Hiroshima Peace Memorial Museum, 9 August 1945.)

広島赤十字病院で 爆心地より1,6km
離れていた広島赤十字病院は、鉄筋コ
ンクリートで火災からは免れたが、医
師・職員・看護婦ら554名のうち、
51名が死亡。250名が傷つき、医療
活動可能な医師はわずか6名、看護婦
は10名であった。ここに1万人以上の
被爆者が殺到。必死の応急治療にあた
ったが、病院は次々と運び込まれる被
爆者で埋め尽くされた。(撮影／1945
年8月10日・宮武甫 提供／朝日新聞
社)

At Hiroshima Red Cross Hospital.
The hospital was 1,6kilometers from
ground zero. Built of reinforced
concrete, the building survived the
fires, but of the 554 doctors, nurses,
and workers employed there, 51
perished and 250 were injured. Only
six doctors and ten nurses were fit for
service. The hospital was flooded
with over 10,000 atomic bomb victims
seeking treatment. The staff worked
valiantly to provide emergency
treatment, but the hospital was soon
overflowing with the casualties
transported there. (Photo by Miyatake
Hajime, provided courtesy of the
Asahi Shimbun Newspaper, 10
August 1945.)

生ましめんかな　　栗原貞子

こわれたビルディングの地下室の夜だった。
原子爆弾の負傷者たちは
ローソク一本ない暗い地下室を
うずめて、いっぱいだった。
生ぐさい血の匂い、死臭。
汗くさい人いきれ、うめきごえ
その中から不思議な声が聞こえて来た。
「赤ん坊が生まれる」と言うのだ。
この地獄の底のような地下室で
今、若い女が産気づいているのだ。
マッチ一本ないくらがりで
どうしたらいいのだろう
人々は自分の痛みを忘れて気づかった。
と、「私が産婆です、私が生ませましょう」
と言ったのは
さっきまでうめいていた重傷者だ。
かくてくらがりの地獄の底で
新しい生命は生まれた。
かくてあかつきを待たず産婆は
血まみれのまま死んだ。
生ましめんかな
生ましめんかな
己が命捨つとも

Bring Forth New Life　　　　**Kurihara Sadako**

It was a night spent in the basement of a burnt out building.
People injured by the atomic bomb took shelter in this room, filling it.
They passed the night in darkness, not even a single candle among them.
The raw smell of blood, the stench of death.
Body heat and the reek of sweat. Moaning.
Miraculously, out of the darkness, a voice sounded:
"The baby's coming!"
In that basement room, in those lower reaches of hell,
A young woman was now going into labor.
What were they to do,
Without even a single match to light the darkness?

People forgot their own suffering to do what they could.
A seriously injured woman who had been moaning but a moment before,
Spoke out:
"I'm a midwife. Let me help with the birth."
And new life was born
There in the deep, dark depths of hell.
Her work done, the midwife did not even wait for the break of day.
She died, still covered with the blood.
Bring forth new life!
Even should it cost me my own,
Bring forth new life!

くりはら・さだこ（1913〜）広島市生まれ。詩人・歌人。被爆直後、爆心地より4kmの自宅から入市。戦後すぐに夫・唯一と「中国文化」を創刊。以後今日まで文学を通した反核運動に積極的に参加。詩集に『栗原貞子詩集』『ヒロシマというとき』などがある。

Kurihara Sadako (1913 ~). This poet, native to Hiroshima, left her home, located 4 kilometers from ground zero, shortly after the bomb was dropped and travelled into the city. Soon after the war ended she began publishing the journal *Chugoku Bunka* with her husband, Tadaichi, and she continues to be active in the anti-nuclear movement through her literary efforts. Her published work includes *Poems by Kurihara Sadako* and *When We Say "Hiroshima."*

爆心地・島病院の尋ね人　被爆時、不在だった院長名で、患者やその家族・病院関係者の消息を尋ねる立て札が出されていた。（撮影／林重男　提供／広島平和記念資料館）

Seeking survivors at the Shima Clinic, ground zero.　Signed by the clinic's director, who was elsewhere at the time of the bombing, this message board asks for news of patients, their families, and the clinic staff. (Photo by Hayashi Shigeo, provided courtesy of Hiroshima Peace Memorial Museum.)

瀬戸物屋跡の消息札　猿楽町にあった大きな瀬戸物屋跡に、1人死亡、5人行方不明、生存2人の所在地が記されていた。（撮影／林重男　提供／広島平和記念資料館）

Message board at a ceramic dealer.　This board, left in the ruins of a large ceramic retailer in Sarugaku-chô, records one fatality, five persons unaccounted for, and the whereabouts of two survivors. (Photo by Hayashi Shigeo, provided courtesy of Hiroshima Peace Memorial Museum.)

絶望を越えて

Transcending Despair

　原爆砂漠のなかで、命をとりとめた人たちは、重度の火傷や放射能障害とたたかっていた。それは虚脱感とのたたかいでもあった。失った家族への涙や傷つく息子や娘への愛が渦巻いていた。

　心の亀裂や肉体的苦痛にあえぎながらも、「人間」を取り戻す営みを生きていた。

In this atomic wasteland those who escaped with their lives battled severe burn injuries and the effects of radiation exposure. The overwhelming exhaustion they struggled with was emotional as well as physical: the grief over loved ones lost and the concern for injured children was palpable.

Though residents were in a state of shock from the emotional and physical pain, the work of restoring something human to this landscape was soon underway.

医師を求めて　重傷の被爆者を抱えた人びとは、医師を求めて街をさまよった。（撮影／1945年10月中旬・菊池俊吉）

In search of a doctor. People roamed the city, often with the most severely injured in tow, looking for medical help. (Photo by Kikuchi Shunkichi , mid-October 1945.)

治療を受けて帰途につく親子　爆心地より4,2kmの宇品町で。母と娘は 負傷し、車を押す父親も腕に火傷している。（撮影／1945年8月中旬・宮武甫 提供／朝日新聞社）

Family on its way home after treatment. In this photo, taken in Ujina-machi (4,2 kilometers from ground zero), a father suffering burns on his arms pushes his injured wife and daughter home. (Photo by Miyatake Hajime, provided courtesy of the Asahi Shimbun Newspaper, mid-August 1945.)

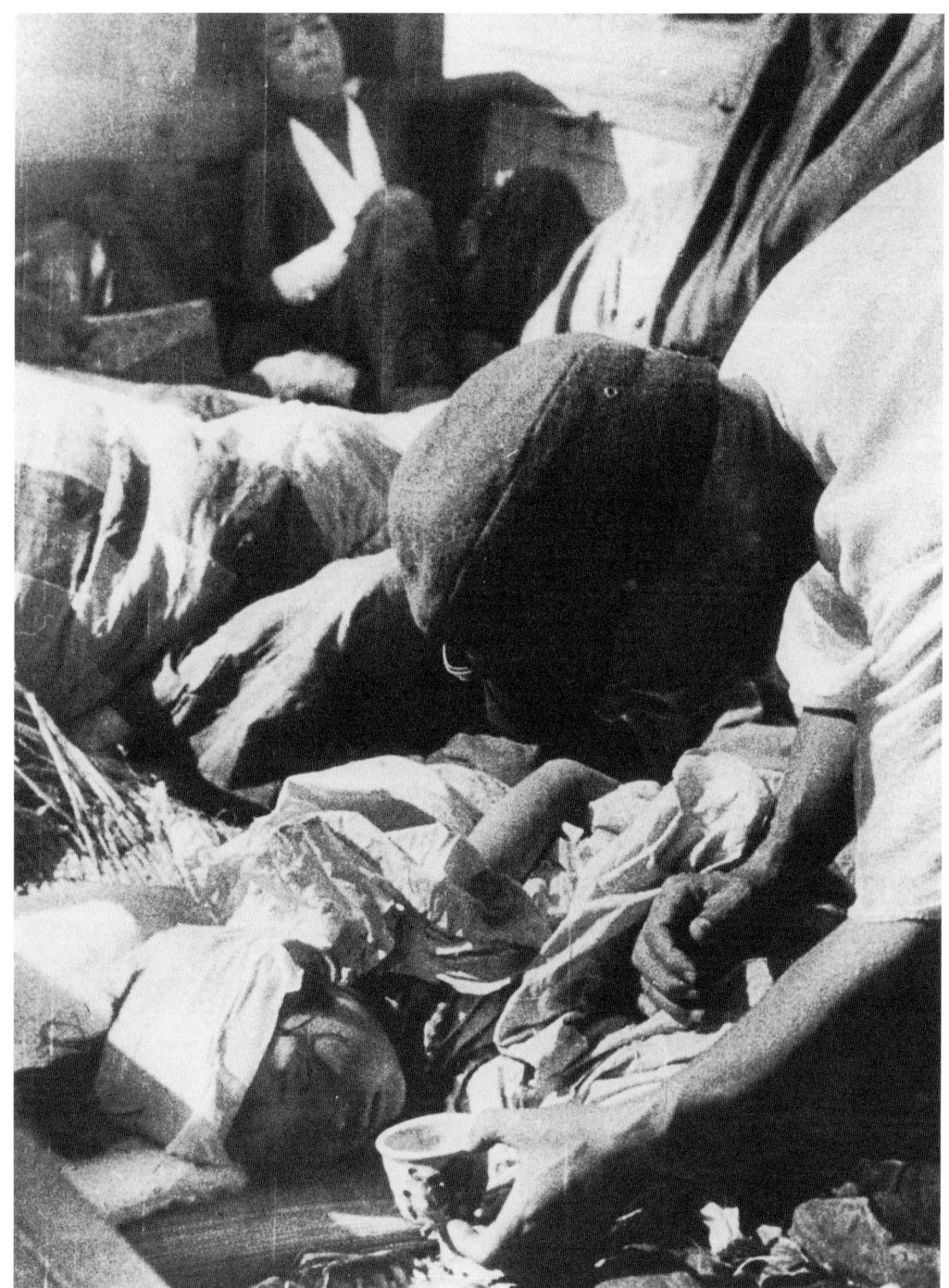

水を差し出される女の子 すでに水を
飲もうともせず、泣き叫ぶ気力も失せ
ているように見えた。（撮影／1945年
8月・宮武甫 提供／朝日新聞社）

Girl being offered a drink of water.
Not even attempting to drink the
water given her, this girl seems to
have lost even the strength to cry out
in pain. (Photo by Miyatake Hajime,
provided courtesy of the Asahi
Shimbun Newspaper, August 1945.)

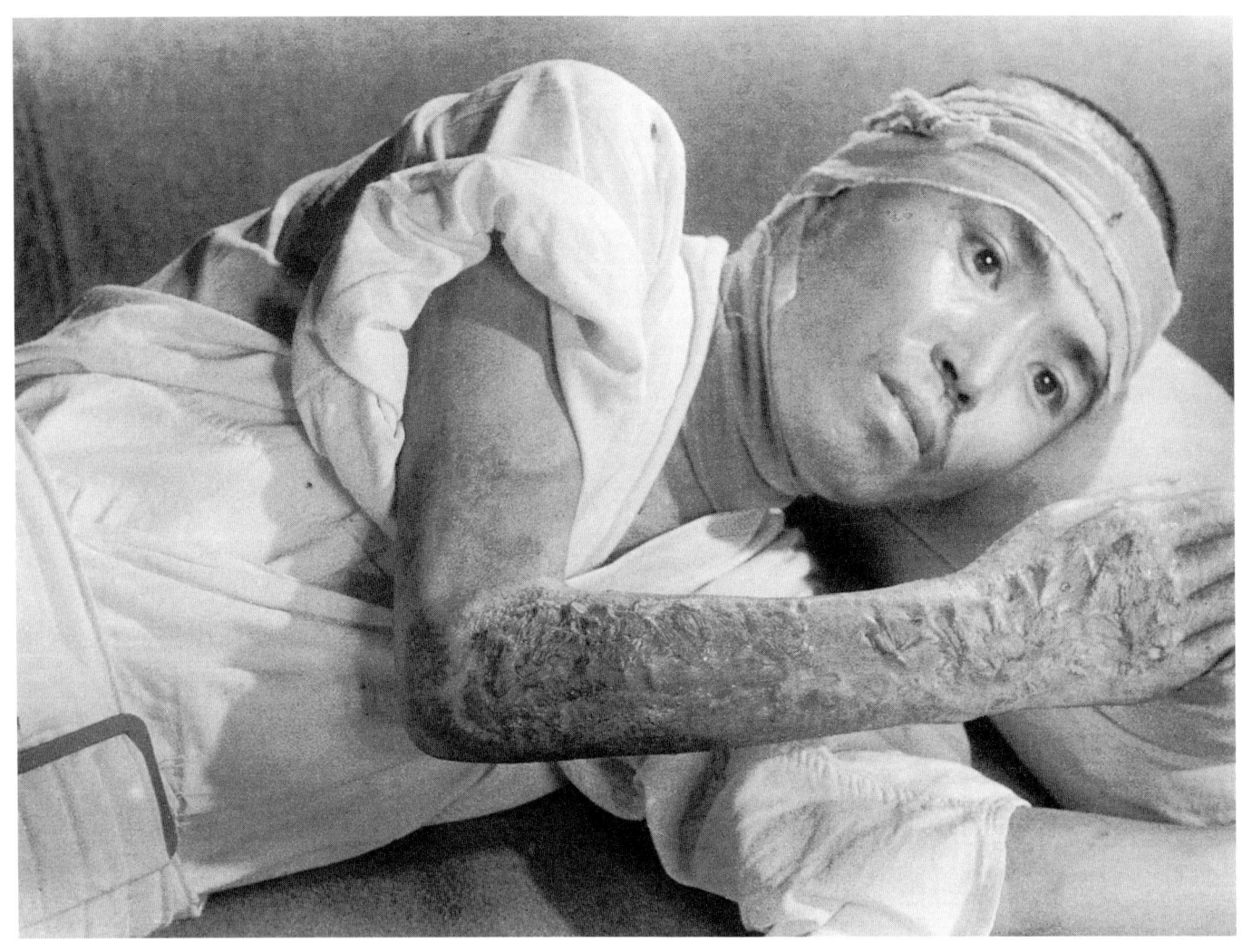

植皮手術を受ける 爆心地より2kmの
千田町で被爆した。右手に大火傷。右
大腿部から植皮の手術を受けるが、原
爆火傷の植皮は放射能の影響もあり、
成功することが難しいという。（撮影／
菊地俊吉）

Skin grafts. This individual was in
Senda-machi, 2 kilometers from
ground zero, when the bomb was
dropped. Though skin from the thigh
has been grafted onto the severely
burned right arm, the effects of the
radiation significantly lower the
chances that such grafts will take.
(Photo by Kikuchi Shunkichi.)

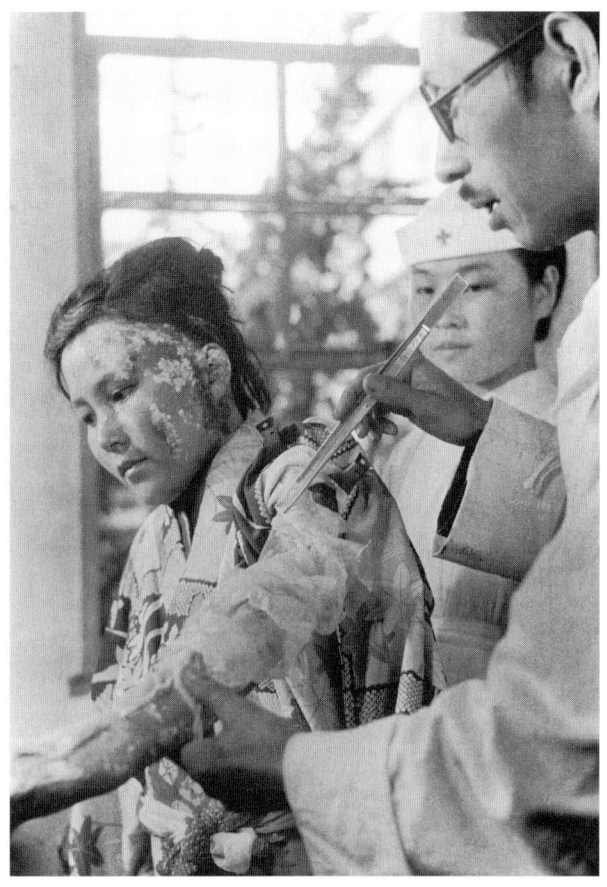

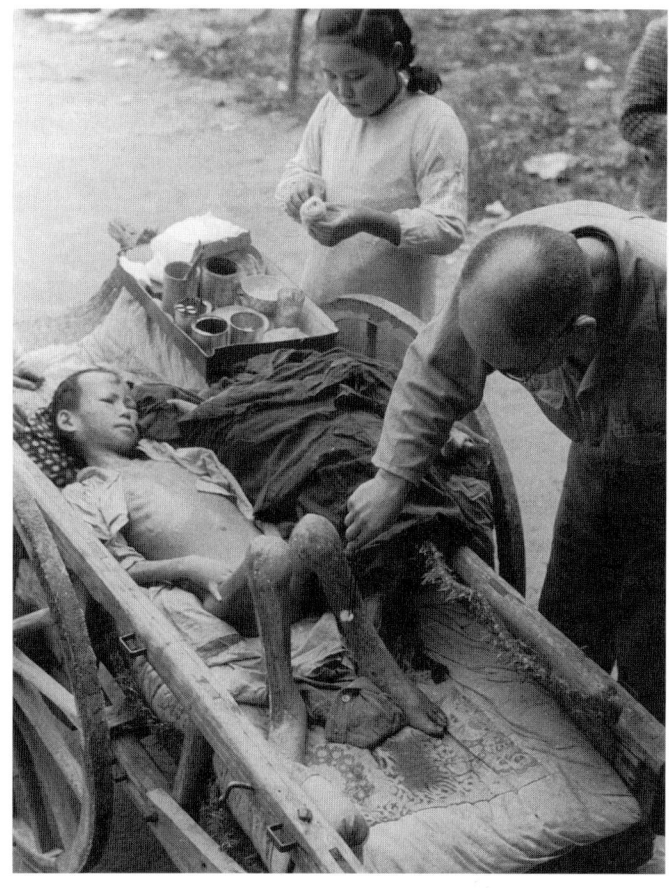

左から浴びた熱線の傷　痛々しい傷は
なかなか癒えない。広島赤十字病院で。
（撮影／1945年10月4日・菊池俊吉）

Burns on the left side from
exposure to the heat rays.　These
painful injuries seemed never to fully
heal.　(Photo by Kikuchi Shunkichi,
Hiroshima Red Cross Hospital, 4
October 1945.)

両足に熱線を浴びた少年　大芝国民学
校に急設された臨時救護病院に治療を
受けにきた。（撮影／菊池俊吉）

Boy burned on both legs.　This boy
came for treatment at the first-aid
station set up at the public school at
Oshiba.　(Photo by Kikuchi Shunkichi.)

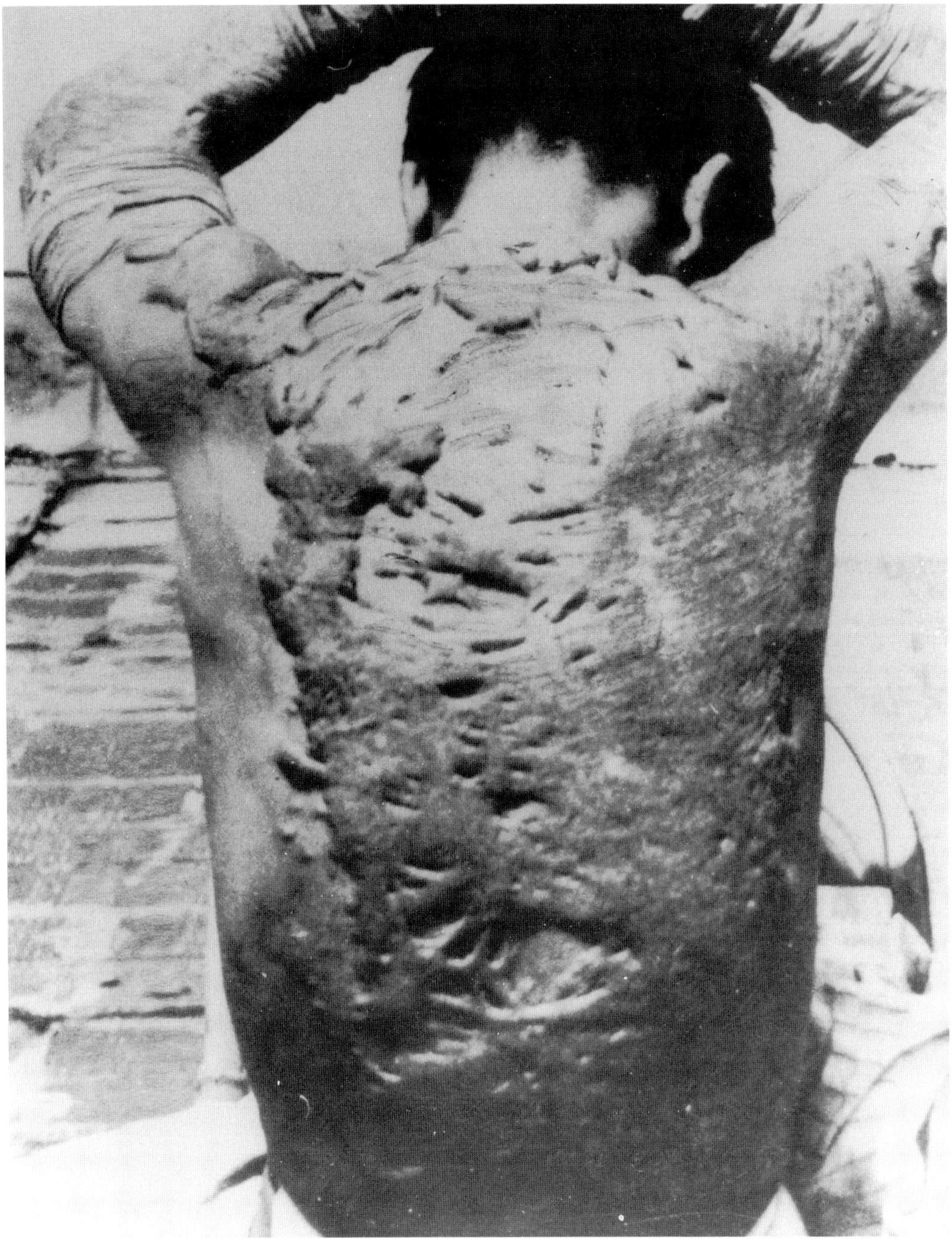

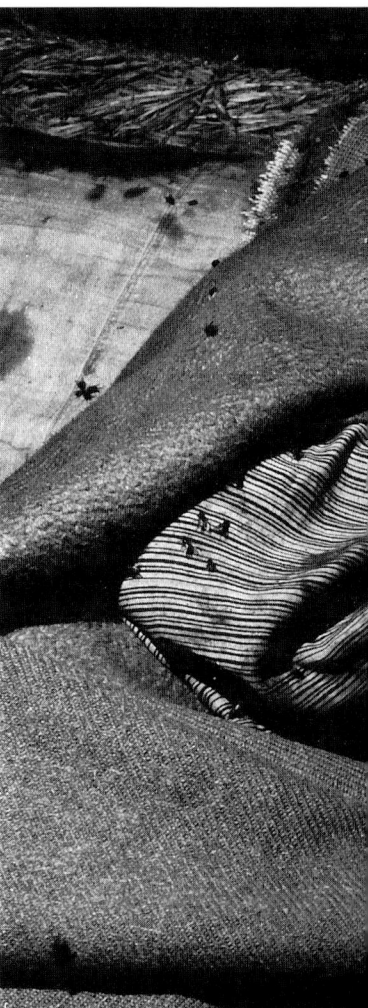

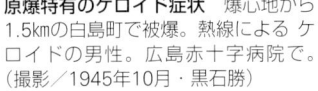

原爆特有のケロイド症状　爆心地から
1.5kmの白島町で被爆。熱線による ケ
ロイドの男性。広島赤十字病院で。
（撮影／1945年10月・黒石勝）

Keloids unique to atomic bomb
victims. This man suffers from
keloids brought on by the heat rays
he was exposed to in Hakushimacho,
1.5 kilometers from ground zero.
(Photo by Kuroishi Masaru, at
Hiroshima Red Cross Hospital,
October 1945.)

老婆に群がる蝿　傷口にウジがわき、
横たわる老婆に蝿が群がる。ただじ
っと耐えるだけの「生」。（撮影／
1945年9月中旬・アメリカ海軍写真
班提供／平和博物館を創る会）

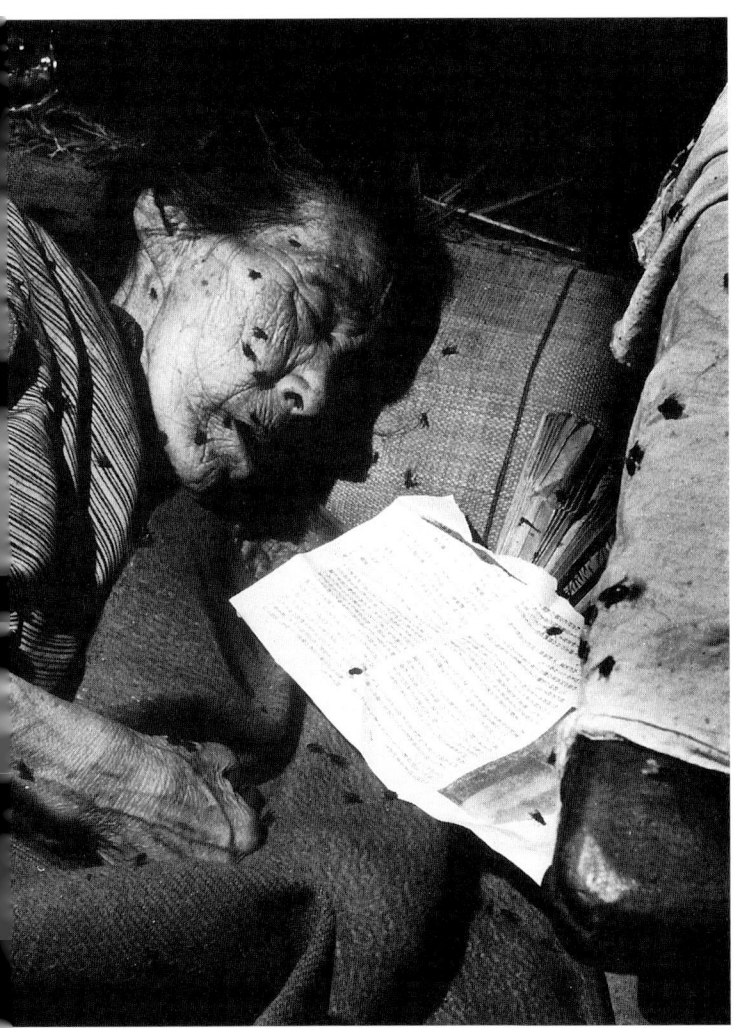

Flies swarming around an elderly woman. Her wounds infested with maggots, this woman is also plagued by swarms of flies as she lies in bed. Her "life" consists of nothing but quietly bearing the pain. (Photo by the U.S. Navy Photographers, provided courtesy of Association to Establish the Japan Peace Museum, mid-September 1945.)

放射能障害で脱毛した姉弟　姉11歳、弟9歳。爆心地からおよそ1kmの船入町の自宅で被爆。2人仲良く宿題をしていた時だった。2人はおよそ2か月目から髪の毛が抜け始め、広島赤十字病院で治療した結果、一時的に髪もはえ、回復したようにみえたが、1949年に弟が死亡。姉は結婚して1児をもうけたが、1965年に原爆症で死亡した。（撮影／1945年10月・菊池俊吉）

Siblings left bald by the radiation. This sister, age 11, and her younger brother, age 9, were happily doing their homework in their house in Funairi-cho, approximately 1 kilometer from ground zero, when the bomb was dropped. They began to lose their hair about two months after the bombing, and received treatment at Hiroshima Red Cross Hospital. Though their hair grew back and they seemed, for a time, to have recovered, the brother died in 1949 and the sister succumbed to atomic bomb sickness in 1965, after having married and given birth to a child. (Photo by Kikuchi Shunkichi, October 1945.)

弔い祈る

Prayers for the Dead

　広島では、祈り・弔いは不戦・平和の誓いである。8月6日午前8時15分の黙祷だけで終わらせてはならないと――。核兵器廃絶のための不断の「行動」をこそ、ヒロシマは世界に向けて呼び掛けている。

Prayers murmured and rites offered in Hiroshima are all vows to oppose war and work for peace. Observing a moment of silence annually on 6 August at 8:15 a.m. is not enough. Hiroshima calls to the world to join it in constant action directed at abolishing nuclear weapons.

似島の千人塚　被爆後、広島市内から似島に逃れた人の多くが、この地で息絶えた。陸軍検疫所に設置された臨時救護所での死亡者も、荼毘に付され、そのまま氏名の確認なく埋葬された。（撮影／1945年10月17日・菊池俊吉）

The grave of the unknown thousands on Ninoshima island. Many of the people who fled Hiroshima for Ninoshima island after the bombing breathed their last in that locale. Those who died in the first-aid station set up at the army quarantine facilities there were cremated and their remains buried before their identities could be confirmed. (Photo by Kikuchi Shunkichi, 17 October 1945.)

刻まれた「原爆死」

　原爆犠牲者の13回忌にあたる1957年夏、写真家・土門拳はカメラを手にする者の使命感にかられて広島に入り、翌年写真集『ヒロシマ』を刊行する。土門はこの写真について次のように記す。

──「椎田家之墓」とある墓には、「裏面に昭和三十二年四月 建之」、左側面に「昭和二十年八月十四日 原爆死 信一 五十三才、昭和二十年八月十五日 原爆死 妻アイ 五十七才、昭和二十年八月六日 原爆死 節子 十四才」と刻んであって、3人の死者の名前の上に全部「原爆死」と断り書きしてある。おそらく父母と一人の妹を失った兄息子の原爆に対する憎悪が、この「原爆死」という3字にまざまざと見てとれた──

　原爆で亡くなった人びとの、新しい多くの墓を土門のカメラは捉えている。(撮影／1957年夏・土門拳)

Engraved with the phrase "Death by Atomic Bomb." For the special twelfth anniversary of the bombing, photographer Domon Ken felt compelled to visit Hiroshima in 1957, camera in hand. The following year he published his book of photographs, *Hiroshima*. He recorded the following concerning this photograph: "On the back of the Shiida family gravestone was carved 'Erected April 1957.' On the left side, it said: 'Shin'ichi (age 53), death by atomic bomb, 14 August 1945; his wife Ai (age 57), death by atomic bomb, 15 August 1945; Setsuko (age 14), death by atomic bomb, 6 August 1945.' The phrase 'death by atomic bomb' is repeated for each of the three deceased, and in that repetition one can sense the abhorrence towards nuclear weapons held by a surviving eldest son who lost both parents and a younger sister to the bomb."

Domon's camera has captured many of the new graves for people who died from the atomic bomb. (Photo by Domon Ken, summer 1957.)

今も発見される遺骨群 被爆から7年がたった1952年7月、原爆犠牲者の遺骨が次々に発見された。広島市宇品沖の金輪島で29体、安芸郡坂町で216体、千田町の元山中高等女学校で43体。写真は坂町で発見された遺骨で、野ざらしの60体、埋葬されていた156体。被爆当時、軍の臨時救護所があり、収容された被爆者が次々に亡くなった。

　現在も発掘調査が続けられており、2004年8月には、似島で60数体が遺品と共に発見された。（提供／中国新聞社刊『被爆50年写真集　ヒロシマの記録』）

Mass graves still being uncovered.
In July 1952, seven years after the bombing, a great number of atomic bomb victim remains were uncovered: 29 in Kanawajima island, in Hiroshima's Ujina bay; 216 in Saka-cho, Aki-gun; 43 where the Yamanaka Girls High School once stood in Senda-machi. This photograph was taken in Saka-cho, where the remains of sixty were found exposed to the elements and another 156 buried in the earth. The site was home to a first-aid station where many atomic bomb victims died.

Excavations continue to this day. In August 2004 sixty corpses buried with their belongings were uncovered on Ninoshima island. (Provided courtesy of the Chugoku Shimbun Newspaper.)

新しい生き方を

平岡　敬

記憶し、伝え続ける

　世界の核状況は確実に悪化した。

　NPT（核不拡散条約）の差別性に不満をもったインド、パキスタンが核実験を強行しただけでなく、核兵器開発を目論む国も後を絶たず、核の水平拡散が進んでいる。

　一方、米国やロシアは爆発を伴う実験こそしないものの、未臨界実験を繰り返して、核兵器の小型化や性能向上を図っており、この核の垂直拡散も深刻な問題である。

　広島、長崎への原爆投下以後、今日まで核のボタンが押されることはなかった。それはやはりヒロシマ・ナガサキの悲惨な記憶が、大国の指導者や世界の人々の脳裏に刻み込まれていたからに違いない。その意味で、ヒロシマ・ナガサキの「核兵器廃絶」のメッセージの果たした役割は大きかった。

　しかしながら、地球上にはまだ3万発近い核弾頭がある。しかも、この半世紀余の間に多くの戦争があり、今またアフガニスタンに次いでイラクで戦闘が続き、日本も派兵に踏み切った。またロシアでもインドネシアでも流血の惨事が頻発している。

　こう見てくると、ヒロシマ・ナガサキの訴えは残念ながら、核兵器をなくすことも、戦争を防ぐこともできなかったと思わざるを得ない。そこには、日本が「核の傘」の下にいながら、他国に対して「核兵器廃絶」を求めてきた自己矛盾も露呈している。

　テロリズムの脅威が人々を襲う「新しい戦争」の時代にあって、ヒロシマ・ナガサキの訴えは意味を持つのか、という思いすら去来する。

　とはいえ、国際社会は富の偏在、人口爆発、環境破壊、資源の浪費など、多くの困難に直面している。それらはテロの温床であり、平和の障害である。

　また、近代科学は核兵器を生み出し、戦争は人間を狂気に導いてきた。どこの国の人間も、狂気の中で加害者となり、被害者となることを、歴史は示している。核兵器を持ってしまった人類が、その狂気から逃れることができるという保証はない。

　このような問題に取り組んで、平和な世界を実現するには、あらゆる国の軍事費の大幅な削減と、時代をリードする階層の人々の利己的な欲望の自制しかない。

　人間の利己的な欲望と狂気の暴走を防ぐためには、核時代における新しい倫理を打ち立てなければならない。その原点となるのが、ヒロシマ・ナガサキの惨劇である。私たちはそれを記憶し、伝え続けることによってのみ、人間を退廃から救うことができる。

国際世論の高まりを目ざして

　被爆60年を機に、広島では被爆体験の継承と共に、あらためて世界の人々、とくにアジアの人々との連帯を求める活動が活発になっている。それは国際世論の力によって、行きづまっている核廃絶への展望を切り開こうとするものである。例えば、韓国の原爆被爆者の渡日治療を支援している組織、セミパラチンスクの核実験被害者への医療援助を続ける市民団体、カンボジアの首都プノンペンに交流拠点「ひろしまハウス」を建設中のグループ、さらにはイラクの劣化ウラン弾被曝者に救援の手を差し伸べる人たち、インド、パキスタンの青少年との交流を通じて平和への道を探る試みなどである。

　アジアに照準を定めたこれらの行動は、「原爆投下によってアジアは解放された」というアジアの多くの人たちの原爆観を正そうとするものであると同時に、広島被爆後、内外から受けた援助への感謝の気持ちの表現でもある。

　広島市民は、自らが悲惨な体験をしたからこそ、他人の痛みを理解することができる。その痛みを共有することによって、人間とは何か、平和とは何か、ということを確かめているのである。

　このような市民の活動は、広島市の「原爆展」開催とも相まって、核廃絶へ向けての国際世論づくりをめざしている。国際世論の高まりこそ、各国の核兵器依存の政策を変えさせ、人類の未来に希望をもたらすからである。

ひらおか・たかし　1927年生まれ。広島県出身。1952年、中国新聞社に入社し、取締役編集局長、中国放送代表取締役社長を歴任。広島県文化財保護委員、広島市教育委員会委員などを経て、1991年2月広島市長に当選。1999年まで2期務める。著書に『偏見と差別』（未来社）、『希望のヒロシマ』（岩波書店）など多数がある。

A New Way of Life
Hiraoka Takashi

Memory and Its Transmission

Without question, nuclear weapons pose an increasing threat in the world today. Not only have India and Pakistan responded to inequalities in the Non-Proliferation of Nuclear Weapons Treaty (NPT) by pressing forward with nuclear weapons tests of their own, but there seems to be no end to the list of countries seeking to develop nuclear capabilities. The nuclear horizon is expanding.

Vertical proliferation is also a serious concern. While on the one hand the United States and Russia have forsworn experiments that include detonation, on the other hand they continue to run tests below critical mass and explore ways to improve the efficiency and decrease the size of nuclear weapons.

It is true that since the atomic bombs were dropped on Hiroshima and Nagasaki, nobody has pushed the nuclear button. Surely this thanks to the fact that both the leaders of powerful nations and people around the world remain keenly aware of the horrors of Hiroshima and Nagasaki. In this sense, these cities have played an important role in the movement for the abolition of nuclear weapons.

And yet there remain almost 30,000 nuclear warheads on the earth today, and the last half century has seen an endless string of wars. Even now, after the war in Afghanistan, there is military action in Iraq, where Japan has taken the significant step of deploying troops. Russia and Indonesia, too, are the scenes of frequent bloodshed.

Taking these facts into consideration, we cannot but conclude that, regrettably, the appeals issued by Hiroshima and Nagasaki have gone largely unheeded; they have neither eliminated nuclear weapons nor prevented war. Contributing to this failure is the internally inconsistent stance of Japan, which calls for the abolition of nuclear weapons in other nations while simultaneously itself remaining under the nuclear umbrella of the United States.

One might also question the pertinence of the pleas of Hiroshima and Nagasaki for an age when warfare often means the terrorist threat against ordinary people. This terrorism is born from the very challenges faced by the international community: the uneven distribution of wealth, the population explosion, ecological devastation, and the wasteful consumption of natural resources. These issues, too, pose an obstruction to peace.

In short, the fact is that we live today in a world where modern science has produced the atomic bomb and war has led humankind into a state of insanity. Furthermore, history teaches us that in this state of insanity all humans, regardless of their nationality, are potential aggressors and potential victims. There is no guarantee that humanity will survive the madness invoked by the nuclear weapons they have created.

Addressing these problems and realizing peace in the world requires two things: the drastic reduction of military budgets across the globe and the exercise of restraint on the selfish desires of influential leaders. A further descent into nuclear madness through the indulgence of self-serving desires can only be prevented by establishing a new ethics for the nuclear age. This ethics would be grounded in the tragedies of Hiroshima and Nagasaki for it is only by preserving and conveying the memory of what occurred there that we can save humankind from ruin.

Towards Increased World Awareness

As the sixtieth anniversary of the atomic bombing approaches, people in Hiroshima have increased their efforts both to preserve the legacy of the bombing and to establish solidarity with people throughout the world, particularly in Asia. They are inspired by a desire to tap the power of international awareness and thereby open new potentials that will break the gridlock in the movement to abolish nuclear weapons. This work is being done by many, including an organization backing medical treatment in Japan for Korean victims of the bomb, a citizen's group providing medical support for victims of atomic weapons tests in Semipalatinsk, an association hoping to facilitate international dialogue by building the "Hiroshima House" in the Cambodian capital of Phnom Penh, the people reaching out to Iraqi victims of depleted uranium munitions, and a project attempting to smooth the road to peace by promoting interaction between Indian and Pakistani youth. These efforts have been directed at Asia in hopes of correcting the mistaken belief that Asia was somehow liberated by the dropping of the atomic bombs; they are also an expression of appreciation for the aid given Hiroshima after the bombing by organizations domestic and abroad.

The people of Hiroshima can empathize with the suffering of others because they themselves have experienced the unthinkable. Such shared experiences of suffering prompt us to reaffirm our beliefs about what it means to be human and what it is that leads to peace.

The activities of these citizens' groups, like the opening of the "Hiroshima Atomic Bomb Exhibit," are intended to build an international consensus on the need to rid the world of nuclear weapons. Such increased world awareness has both the power to change the politics of nations dependent on nuclear weapons and the power to bring to humankind once again true hope for the future.

Hiraoka Takashi . Born in Hiroshima in 1927, Hiraoka joined The Chugoku Newspaper Company in 1952. After serving as president and editor-in-chief for that firm and as CEO of Chugoku Broadcasting Services, he sat on the Committee for the Preservation of Hiroshima Prefecture's Culture and the Hiroshima City Board of Education. He was elected mayor in February 1991, serving two terms lasting to 1999. He has numerous books to his name, including *Henken to sabetsu* (Prejudice and discrimination, Miraisha Publishing) and *Kibo no Hiroshima* (Hiroshima of hope, Iwanami Shoten Publishing).

長
NAGASAKI
崎

爆心地付近の惨状 "原爆荒野"と化した被爆地で、石の鳥居だけが不思議に原型をとどめていた。（撮影／1945年8月10日・山端庸介）

　山端庸介（1917～1966）は長崎が被爆した時、西部軍報道班員嘱託として東京から福岡に配属されていた。被爆情報を受けた軍は、長崎の状況を把握する必要から山端を含む3人に、即座に視察命令を下した。
　平時6時間半の博多から長崎160kmを、12時間かかって浦上にたどり着いたのは、10日午前3時だった。

　山端は、こうして8月10日、被爆直後の長崎の現実を撮った。丸1日調査を続けた3人は、午後5時の列車で長崎を去った。
　この時の映像は『記録写真 原爆の長崎』として刊行される1952年夏まで、占領軍の意思で封印されたままだった。

ナガサキ　二重の悲劇

　1945年8月9日午前11時2分、軍需工場が密集する長崎市上空に達したB29戦略爆撃機は、実戦配備された2発目の核兵器（プルトニウム型原爆、通称「ファットマン」＝長さ3.2m、直径1.5m、重さ4.5t）を投下した。一瞬にして、浦上川の流域から長崎湾にかけて発展してきた長崎市の大半がこの原爆によって壊滅させられた。（巻末の長崎被爆地図参照）

　死者約7万人（1945年末まで）、そしてそれとほぼ同数の「被爆者」を生み出したこの「ナガサキ」の被害は、すでに「終わっていた」戦争に使用された2発目の核兵器として、また当初の投下目的地が長崎ではなく小倉であったという事実において、被害の規模はヒロシマより小さかったにもかかわらず、二重の悲劇を体現するものであったといえるだろう。

　そして、ナガサキの場合、その惨劇にあった人びとのなかに、長崎の地に長く暮らす中国人や捕虜となっていたイギリス人、オーストラリア人など日本人でない国籍を持つ人が数多くいたということは、この大量破壊兵器＝原爆が「敵」に属する都市や人びとを破壊し殺戮するだけではなく、人種や国境を易々と越え、「人間」存在の本質と敵対する究極の兵器であることを物語っていた。ナガサキは、その典型＝原型を示したのである。

Nagasaki: The Tragedy Repeated

In the morning on 9 August 1945 a B29 strategic bomber reached the skies over Nagasaki, a city which had started in the Urakami River basin and spread out to the shores of the bay. At 11:02 a.m. the bomber dropped the second deployable nuclear weapon, a plutonium bomb nicknamed "Fat man," the bomb was 3.2 meters in length, 1.5 meters in diameter, and it weighed 4.5 tons. In an instant most of Nagasaki, a city dense with munitions factories, was destroyed.

(Please refer to the "Nagasaki Atomic Bomb Map" included at the back of this volume.)

By the close of 1945 the bomb had claimed approximately 70,000 fatalities and an almost equal number of casualties. Though the catastrophe did not reach the proportions of Hiroshima, this was true only because Nagasaki had been substituted at the last moment for Kokura, the original target. Nevertheless, the deployment of this second nuclear weapon at a point where the war was essentially already over represents a duplication of the tragedy.

Among the victims of the Nagasaki atomic bombing were numerous non-Japanese, including long-term Chinese residents as well as English and Australian prisoners-of-war. Their deaths illustrate how weapons of mass destruction such as the atomic bomb not only destroy cities and massacre humans in the "enemy" camp, but also how they transcend all boundaries of race and nation to target the very essence of human existence. Nagasaki is an archetypal example of this fact.

Devastation in the vicinity of ground zero. In the wasteland created by the atomic bomb, only this stone *torii*, the gateway to a shrine, retains by some miracle its original shape. (Photo by Yamahata Yosuke,10 August 1945.)

Yamahata Yosuke (1917~1966). At the time the atomic bomb was dropped on Nagasaki, Yamahata had already left Tokyo for Fukuoka, where he was on special assignment to the Information Bureau of the western branch of the military. When news of the bomb reached headquarters, they immediately dispatched Yamahata and two others for the reconnaissance of Nagasaki, knowledge of which was deemed essential.

People generally made the 160 kilometers trip from Hakata to Nagasaki in six hours. It took Yamahata's team a full twelve, and they arrived in Urakami, on the northern part of the city, on 10 August at 3 a.m. The three-man team surveyed the city for a full day, and Yamahata's photographs recorded the state of Nagasaki on this day after the bombing. They left the city by train at 5 p.m.

Under orders from the Occupation Forces, Yamahata's photographs were kept under wraps until the summer of 1952, when they were published as *Kiroku shashin: Genbaku no Nagasaki* (Nagasaki and the atomic bomb: A photo documentary).

爆心地・松山町交差点付近の惨状　燃えるものはすべて燃え、原爆特有の屋根瓦が平均した大きさに割れ、散乱していた。左端は同行した画家・山田栄二氏。中央の煙突のある建物は長崎製鋼所。（撮影／1945年8月10日・山端庸介）

Devastation at the Matsuyama-cho intersection, ground zero. Anything combustible was incinerated and the area is carpeted with roofing tiles shattered to roughly the same size, a trademark of the atomic bomb. On the left is Yamada Eiji, the artist accompanying Yamahata. The smokestacks visible to the left of center are the Nagasaki Steel Mill. (Photo by Yamahata Yosuke, 10 August 1945.)

爆心地付近で焼死した少年　（撮影／1945年8月10日・山端庸介）

Boy burned to death near ground zero. (Photo by Yamahata Yosuke, 10 August 1945.)

地を這う老婆　爆心地より南1.2km、
三菱製鋼前の県道で。（撮影／1945年
8月10日・山端庸介）

Elderly woman crawling.　The
location is 1.2 kilometers south of
ground zero, on the highway in front
of the Mitsubishi Steel Mill. (Photo by
Yamahata Yosuke, 10 August 1945.)

若い人たちへ

林　京子

昭和20年——1945年の8月9日から今日まで、私は被爆者として生きてきました。

被爆者として生きてきた実感を、21世紀を生きるあなた方へ書き残します。

私は女学校の3年生のときに、長崎市内にある三菱兵器工場で、学徒動員中に被爆しました。爆心地の松山町から1.4kmの地点です。先日、2004年の8月、爆心地の側にある平和公園を訪ねました。

「訪ねた」——この言葉を書きながら、あの日から遠くにいる私を感じています。なぜなら、平和公園がある場所は、命一つを得て懸命に逃げていた女学生の日の場所ですから。

真夏日が続く街は、夕方になっても日照りが去らず、公園の噴水のまわりには人びとが涼をとっていました。ここにいる人たちのなかで、あの日を知っているのは私一人ぐらいだろう、と思いながら逝った52人の学友や師の御魂に手をあわせて、私もまた、人びとに混じって涼をとりました。

足許には、まるまると太ったハトがお尻をふりながら、土や砂をついばんでいます。公園の下を走る市電の騒音も丘をのぼってきます。何気ない日常の風景ですが、しみじみ有難く思いました。

あれから半世紀以上。その間、私が恐れながら生きてきたことは、原爆症の再発です。9日に受けた放射能、吸い込んでしまった放射性物質が、どのような形で肉体に現れてくるか。また、被爆2世、3世といわれる、私たちが産んだ子どもや、その次の子たちの肉体に、どのような変化をもたらすか。

体内に吸い込んだ放射性物質は、骨などに付着して年月をかけて体内に留まり、ミクロの世界の出来事ですが、絶えず低線量の放射能を放射し、これも20年、30年の歳月をかけて人体に害を及ぼす。このことは『内部の敵』（J・M・グールド、放射線・公衆衛生プロジェクトその他の共著・肥田舜太郎その他の共訳）に記されています。これらは学問的な研究過程ですが、被爆者は生きてきた日々のなかで、「内部の敵」を実感し、目に見えない敵を恐れながら生きてきたのです。被爆者の結婚も、新しい生命の誕生も、祝福されないもので

した。産まれてくる子どもの障害を恐れて、産まないことを結婚の条件にしたクラスメートもいます。流産を繰り返した友人、入退院の末に30代、40代の若さで逝った友人もたくさんいます。

不可解なのは、これらいくつもの事実がありながら、「6日・9日と発病の因果関係は不明」とされることです。仮に被爆に起因した原爆症と診断されても、原爆症の認定は困難です。原爆症らしいが証明はできない。故に「不明」とされて、公の認定は却下されます。

なぜ、認定が必要か。記録して数字に残すためです。数字は、ときによって煩わしい結果を生みますが、原子爆弾、核兵器の恐怖はヒトの種と人間の生命、生きていく肉体に人為的に斑点をつけ、さまざまな害を及ぼす。その証明のために、数字は要ります。却下されて不明なまま死んでいった人びとの死こそ、核兵器の恐ろしさなのです。

穢れのない、輝いている美しい目をもっている若いあなたたち、日本には永久に戦争を放棄する、と明確に記した平和憲法があります。その澄んだ目で、透明な思考で、大事に、大事に平和憲法を守ってください。あなた自身のために。産まれてくる新しい生命のために。お願いします。

はやし・きょうこ　1930年8月、長崎市生まれ。小説家。少女期、父の勤務地の中国・上海で過ごすが、1945年春、混乱する上海を離れ、故郷に帰国して被爆。1975年、「祭りの場」により芥川賞受賞。以後、「ギヤマン　ビードロ」「トリニティからトリニティへ」など被爆体験を素材とする作品を書き続ける。2005年、全8巻の全集が日本図書センターより刊行される。

A Message to Our Youth   Hayashi Kyoko

Since that day in the twentieth year of Showa (1945), 9 August, I have lived as a *hibakusha*, a victim of the atomic bomb. This essay is a record of how that feels, and I leave it for you who will live deep into the twenty-first century.

I was in my third year of middle school and, having been conscripted for wartime labor, was working in the Mitsubishi munitions factory in Matsuyama-cho, Nagasaki, when the bomb was dropped. I was 1.4 kilometers from ground zero. Not long ago, on a day in August 2004, I visited the Peace Park that now stands beside ground zero.

As I write the word "visited," I realize how far removed I am now from that day in 1945. The park's location is, after all, none other than that from which I fled furiously, my life spared, back on that day when I was still just a student, and I could very well have imagined my recent trip as a "return."

The mid-summer heat of 2004 stretched late into the season, and even into the evening the sun continued to beat down on the city. People were gathered around the fountain in the Peace Park, cooling themselves. "I'm probably the only one among them who was here on that day," I thought, and I put my hands together in prayer for my 52 classmates and the teachers now gone. I then re-joined the crowd cooling itself by the fountain.

There was a plump pigeon at my feet, wiggling its tail feathers as it pecked around in the sand. The clanking of the streetcars passing below reached us in the park on the top of the hill. It was an ordinary, everyday scene, but I was filled with gratitude for being able to experience it.

More than half a century has past, but I have lived every day in fear of a reemergence of the effects of the radiation. We were showered with it that day, we inhaled irradiated particles. How will this physically effect us? What mutations will it prompt in the bodies of the second and third generation *hibakusha*, our children and the generation after them?

Irradiated particles absorbed into the body attach themselves to the bones and remain in the system for months and years on end. Though on a microscopic level, they continue to emit low levels of radiation that are harmful to the human body for twenty or even thirty years. This phenomenon has been chronicled in *The Enemy Within* (Jay M. Gould and the Project on Radiation and the Public Health). This book is a piece of academic research, but the *hibakusha* victims of the bomb experience the "enemy within" in a more direct manner in their daily lives, living in constant fear of this invisible foe. *Hibakusha* marriages and births were no cause for celebration. One classmate, for example, married only on the condition that there be no children; she was afraid of giving birth to a child with birth defects. Other friends of mine have suffered multiple miscarriages, still others have been in and out of hospitals before passing away in their thirties and forties.

What remains incomprehensible to me is that even in the face of such evidence, the experts declare that "the relationship of the illnesses and the events of August sixth and ninth remains unclear." In the rare case that a diagnosis does point to radiation sickness caused by the atomic bomb,

official recognition is still difficult to obtain because, however much the symptoms may point to radiation sickness, the diagnosis is all but impossible to prove. As a result, the cause of the illness is recorded as "unknown," and the government refuses to officially recognize it as caused by the atomic bomb.

Official recognition is necessary because it records the statistics for posterity. The horror of the atomic bomb and nuclear weapons lies in their unnatural interference in the process of reproduction, in the life of human beings, and in the living organism that is the body. The damage done is wide-ranging and so, though statistics often lead to spurious conclusions, this is one case where numeric evidence is absolutely crucial. Nothing is more frightening about the bomb than the fact that it sends people to deaths that are not acknowledged for what they truly are.

Let me remind you young people, your beautiful eyes gleaming with innocence, that Japan possesses a constitution of peace that explicitly denounces war for all time. I ask you to protect that constitution by exercising unclouded vision and clear thinking. I ask this for your sake, and for the sake of the as-yet unborn. I ask this of you.

Hayashi Kyoko. Born in Nagasaki in August 1930, Hayashi is a novelist. Her father's work took her to Shanghai, China, where she spent much of her childhood. Turmoil there in the spring of 1945 took the family back to their hometown of Nagasaki, where they became victims of the bomb. Hayashi won the Akutagawa Prize, a prestigious literary award, for her 1975 novel *Matsuri no ba* (Ritual of death). She has since published many works based on her experience of the bomb, including *Gyaman biidoro* (Cut glass, blown glass), and *Toriniti kara toriniti e* (From Trinity to Trinity). A collection of her works in seven volumes is forthcoming in 2005.

学徒　　　　中川美苗

動員学徒の友達は
山こえ　谷こえ、生きのがれ
次々　黄色の水吐いて
とうとう動けなくなった
時々　しゃがんで行く友が
だんだん小さくなってゆく
だんだん遠くなってゆく
ふりかえり　ふりかえり　あゝあゝ

The Students　　　Nakagawa Minae

Friends, conscripted for labor while still students,
Fled for their lives, crossing mountains, crossing valleys.
Then, one after the next, they vomited yellow,
And eventually fell still.
One friend pressed on, at times doubling over in pain,
Growing smaller and smaller in the distance,
Looking back, looking back. Aah, aah.

なかがわ・みなえ（1928〜）県立長崎高等女学校在学中、学徒動員先の軍事工場で被爆。1980年、ＮＨＫ長崎放送局が市民に呼び掛け刊行した『長崎原爆の歌』（147編収録）に応募した作品。

Nakagawa Minae (1928〜). while a student at a Nagasaki girl's school, was involved in the student mobilization and working at a military factory when the atomic bomb was dropped. In 1980 the Nagasaki branch of NHK, Japan's national broadcasting company, solicited poems from local residents for publication in *Nagasaki genbaku no uta* (Poems of the Nagasaki atomic bomb). Nakagawa's poem was one of 147 selected for inclusion.

廃墟と化した浦上天主堂 爆心地より東北東500m。浦上天主堂の南側入口に立つ悲しみの聖母像（左）と聖ヨハネ像（右）。被爆時、2人の神父と20数名の信徒が瓦礫と化した天主堂と運命を共にした。
（撮影／1945年10〜11月・アメリカ戦略爆撃調査団　提供／平和博物館を創る会）

The Urakami Cathedral, turned to ruins. At the southern entrance to the Urakami Cathedral, located 500 meters east-north-east from ground zero, stand statues of a grieving Virgin Mary (left) and the apostle John (right). Two priests and over twenty parishioners shared the sad fate of this cathedral, which was turned to rubble. (Photo by Strategic Bombing Survey U.S., provided courtesy of the Association to Establish the Japan Peace Museum, October/November 1945.)

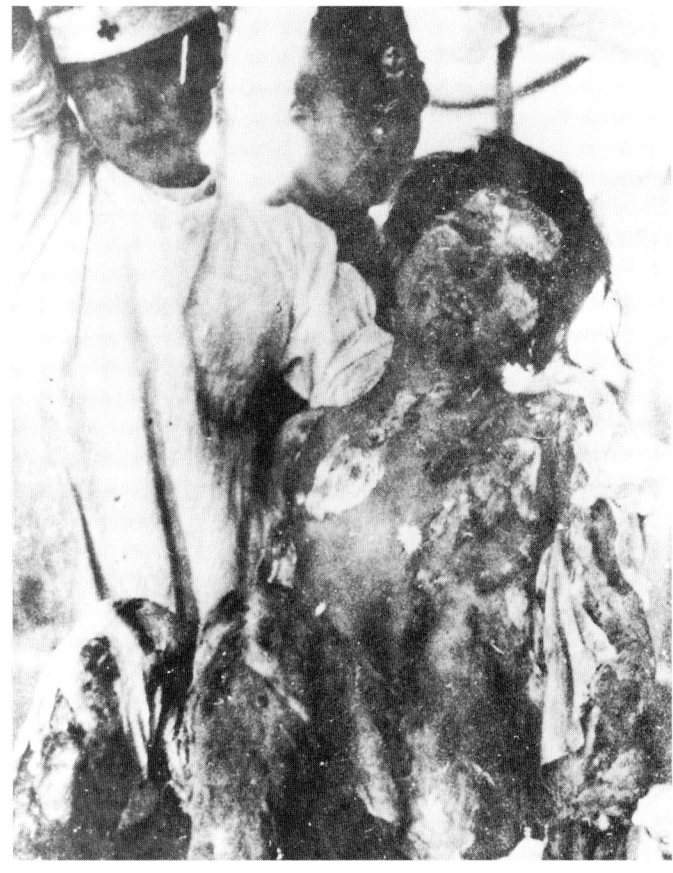

焼死体の傍らに立つ少女　防空壕から脱出しようとして焼死した人。茫然とたたずむ少女はこの時、15歳。後にこの遺体は彼女の母親に違いないとされた。（撮影／1945年8月10日・山端庸介）

Young girl standing beside a charred corpse. The victim died trying to flee from an air-raid dugout. The young girl standing bewildered beside the corpse was fifteen years old at the time. It was later determined that the corpse was that of her mother. (Photo by Yamahata Yosuke, 10 August 1945.)

病院に運び込まれた少女　爆心地より17kmの大村海軍病院（現・国立長崎中央病院）に収容された14歳の少女。全身熱傷に覆われ、ボロボロの皮膚が垂れ下っていた。
（撮影／1945年8月10日頃・塩月正雄）

　塩月さん（1920～1979）は、被爆時25歳の見習い医官で、被爆者の治療にあたるかたわら死亡者の病理解剖を行なう。戦後、東京大学で精神医学、脳外科を研究した。

Young girl carried to a hospital. This young girl, fourteen years old, was admitted to the Omura Naval Hospital (now the National Nagasaki Central Hospital), 17 kilometers from ground zero. She suffered severe burns over her entire body, and her ravaged skin hung loosely. (Photo by Shiotsuki Masao , about 10 August 1945.)

　Mr. Shiotsuki (1920~1979) was a twenty-five year old apprentice medical officer at the time of the bombing. In addition to treating victims of the atomic bomb, he also performed autopsies on those who succumbed to their injuries. After the war he went on to work in psychiatry and brain surgery at Tokyo University's medical school.

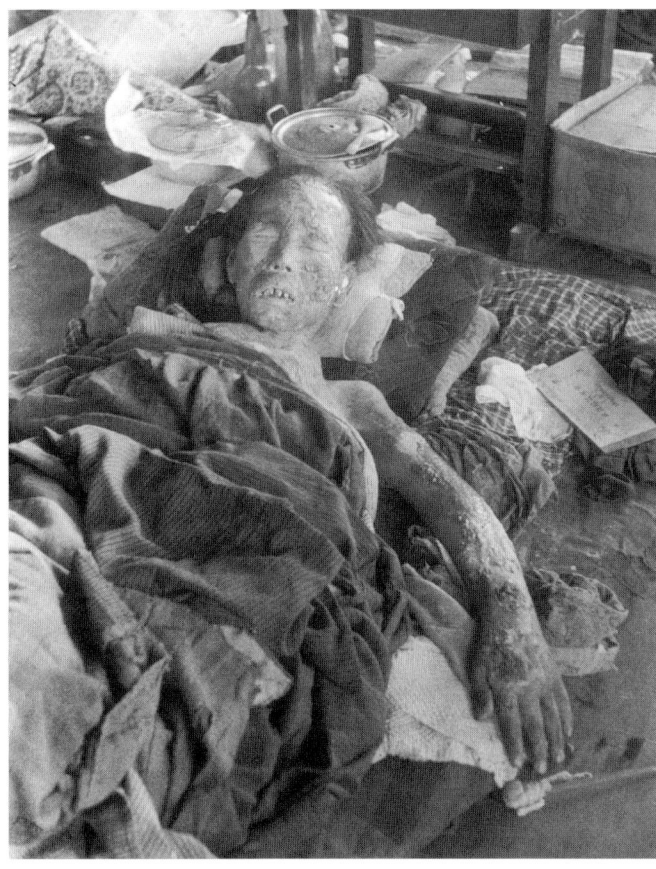

熱傷を負った婦人　新興善臨時救護所で。（撮影／1945年8月下旬・松本栄一）

Woman suffering from burn wounds.　Photo taken at the first aid station at Shinkozen. (Photo by Matsumoto Eiichi, late August 1945.)

路上に倒れた馬　爆心地・松山町付近の道路上で。長崎方面に向かって進行中の荷馬車。倒れた馬の位置が進行方向と逆になっていた。（撮影／1945年8月10日・山端庸介）

Horse collapsed on the road.　This horse had been pulling a wagon in the direction of Nagasaki when the blast killed it on the road near Matsuyama-cho, ground zero.　Its body lies facing away from its destination, apparently turned around by the blast.　(Photo by Yamahata Yosuke, 10 August 1945.)

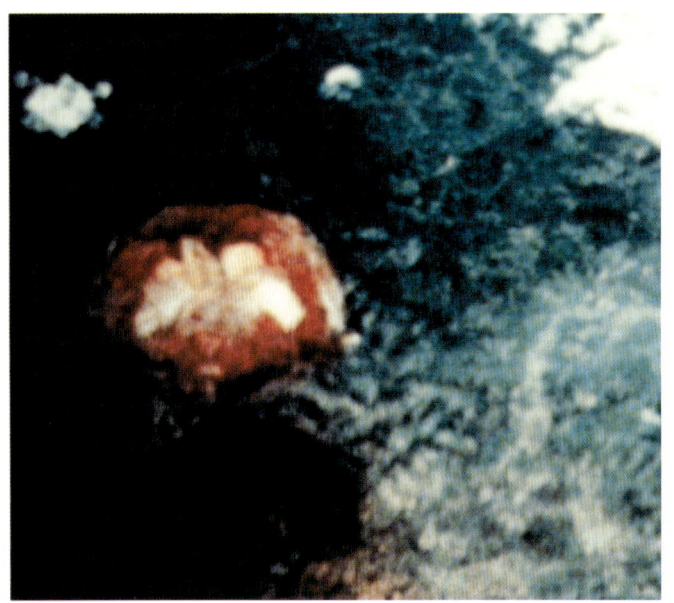

原爆炸裂の瞬間から巨大なキノコ雲が長崎上空を覆うまで　この連続写真は、米軍機の窓越しに撮影された3分50秒の16㎜映画フィルムからコマ撮りしたもの。まず、炸裂の瞬間（p.2の写真）の白い閃光と白雲をとらえると、見る間に真っ赤な火の玉となって膨れ上がる。長崎市内は火の玉の色が反射してか、下方に赤みがかって見える。やがて真っ赤な火球は白いキノコ状の雲になった後、膨らみながら高度を上げる。次いで、どす黒い円筒状の雲が立ちのぼり、上部が白いキノコ状に膨らんで次の傘を生む。数分後には、1万mを越える巨大で不気味なキノコ雲へと成長していった。（米軍撮影　提供／平和博物館を創る会）

The moment of detonation to the formation of a gigantic mushroom cloud covering the skies over Nagasaki. This series of photographs are frames from the three-minute-fifty-second film taken from the window of the American bomber. The first frame (see photo on page 2) captures the moment of detonation, with its blinding flash and white cloud. The photo on the left above shows the instant change to an expanding bright red fireball. The city of Nagasaki below appears red, perhaps reflecting the color of the fireball. The next photo shows the fireball turned into a white mushroom cloud, swelling in size as it gains altitude. Next appear black cylindrical clouds, their tops white and mushroom-shaped. These tops formed the next layer. The final stage, shown in the photo on the following page, shows the expansion of an enormous, ominous mushroom cloud over 10,000 meters across. (Photo by U.S.Army; provided courtesy of the Association to Establish the Japan Peace Museum.)

全焼崩壊した三菱製鋼 長崎駅前から撮った三菱製鋼長崎製鋼所第2工場。爆心地より約1km。三菱製鋼長崎製鋼所の工場群では、被爆当時、動員学徒、女子挺身隊員らを含め、約2,000名が働いていたが、このうちおよそ1,400名が死亡した。（撮影／1945年10月中旬・林重男　提供／広島平和記念資料館）

Burnt ruins of the Mitsubishi Steel Mill. This building, approximately 1 kilometer from ground zero, is plant two of Mitsubishi's Nagasaki steel works as seen from Nagasaki Station. As many as 2,000 employees, including mobilized students and women, were at work in the Mitsubishi compound when the bomb was dropped. Approximately 1,400 of them died. (Photo by Hayashi Shigeo, provided courtesy of Hiroshima Peace Memorial Museum, mid-October 1945.)

母と子の遺体 長崎駅のプラットホームで。写真の黒く見える部分は朱赤色で、原爆火傷である。子どもの顔がハレ上がっている。母親がかけていた白い布は誰かがかけたものであろう。布団を敷いている理由も分からない。（撮影／1945年8月10日午前6〜7時頃　山端庸介）

Corpses of Mother and Child. What appear as dark spots on the bodies in this photo are, in fact, the dark red of burn wounds caused by the atomic bomb. The child's face is severely swollen. The white cloth partially covering the mother was most likely placed there by a passer-by. The presence of the bedding on which the mother rests is inexplicable. (Photo by Yamahata Yosuke, 10 August 1945, between 6 and 7 a.m.)

縁側で被爆死した少年　爆心地から道
ノ尾への間の大きな人家で。家具や建
具は爆風で全部一方に寄り、中はガラ
ンとして空き家のようになり、縁側で
少年がまるで眠るように死んでいた。
（撮影／1945年8月10日・山端庸介）

Young boy killed by the atomic
bomb on his veranda. All of the
furniture and accessories in this large
private residence, somewhere
between ground zero and Michinoo,
have been blown to one side by the
blast, leaving the living space itself
empty, as if the house was vacant.
The boy himself lies dead, looking as
though asleep on the veranda. (Photo
by Yamahata Yosuke, 10 August
1945.)

爆心地付近の惨状 爆心地より南東700mの長崎医科大学付属病院から見た爆心地付近の原爆荒野。手前は山里町（現・平野町）の高台。左遠方の建物は城山国民学校。正面の山は岩屋山。（撮影／1945年10〜11月・アメリカ戦略爆撃調査団 提供／平和博物館を創る会）

Devastation in the area of ground zero. The view from the Nagasaki Medical College Hospital, located 700 meters to the south-east of ground zero, reveals the wasteland created by the atomic bomb. In the foreground are the hills of Yamazato-machi (the current Hirano-machi); the building on the left in the distance is the Shiroyama People's School; in the background is Mt. Iwaya. (Photo by Strategic Bombing Survey U.S., provided courtesy of Association to Establish the Japan Peace Museum, October/November 1945.)

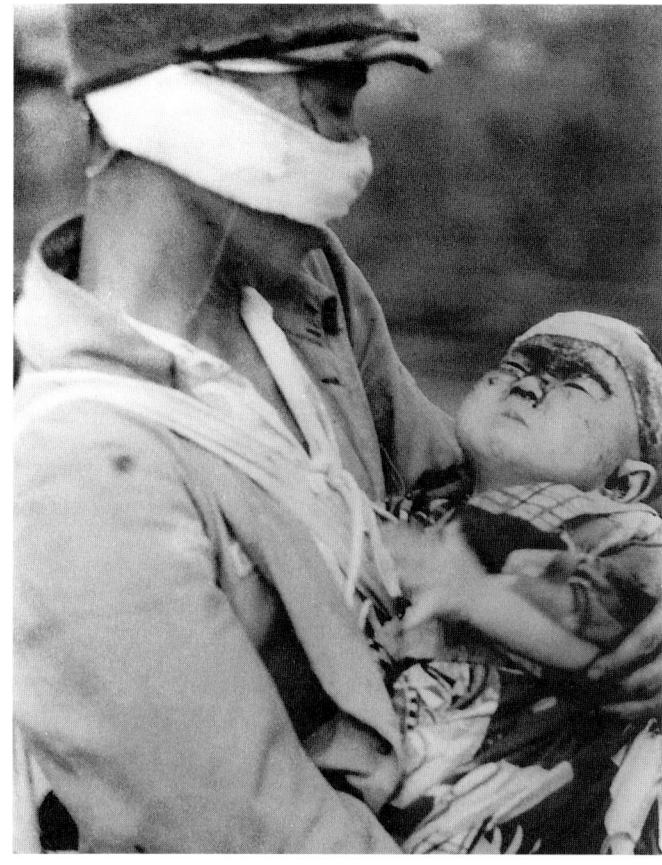

水を飲む少女　一面焦土と化したなか、炎天の太陽と地熱を避けようとして、10名ほどの負傷者が破壊されたトラックの日陰に倒れ伏していた。…市の連絡員がもってきた少量の水筒の水を回し飲みしている。爆心地より約1.1km、井樋ノ口付近で。（撮影／1945年8月10日午前10時頃・山端庸介）

Young girl drinking water. With nothing but scorched earth as far as the eye can see, ten injured victims of the bomb escape the blazing sun and the hot earth by stretching out in the shade of a burned-out truck. Here in the area of Ibinokuchi, 1.1 kilometers from ground zero, they passed around a small water bottle delivered by city rescue workers. (Photo by Yamahata Yosuke, 10 August 1945, approximately 10 a.m.)

父に抱かれた乳飲み子　長崎駅付近で。泣く元気もない乳飲み子と医師を探す父親。（撮影／1945年8月10日午後2時頃・山端庸介）

Infant held by its father. In the area around Nagasaki Station, this father searches for a doctor for his baby, too weak to even cry. (Photo by Yamahata Yosuke, 10 August 1945, approximately 2 p.m.)

おにぎりをもつ母子 井樋ノ口救護本部で、炊き出しのおにぎりをもらった。生き残った母親からの後の聞き取りによると、長崎県五島列島の出身で、被爆時29歳。4人の子どもをもつ母親だった。写真の子どもは、2人の姉と1人の妹がいる男の子で、当時3歳。爆心地から1.6km南の自宅は全壊。割れ飛ぶガラスを頭部に浴びた。戦後、彼女は行商をして、鍋・釜を作る夫と共に一家の暮らしを支える。その後、男の子は工業高校を卒業し、父親と造船の下請け工場を経営。その後、結婚して2人の子どもにも恵まれたが、父親は放射能の後遺症に苦しみながら1983年に亡くなった。母親は1991年、息子たちに見守られながら74歳の生涯を終えた。（撮影／1945年8月10日・山端庸介）

Mother and son with rice balls. They received these freshly cooked rice balls at the first-aid headquarters at Ibinokuchi. The mother, who survived, later reported that she was originally from the Goto Islands to the northwest of Nagasaki City, and twenty-nine at the time of the bombing. A mother of four, she is here accompanied by her three year old son. His three sisters, two elder and one younger, are not present. Their head injuries were caused by flying glass as their home, 1.6 kilometers south of ground zero, came crashing down. After the war, to support the family, this woman peddled goods while her husband made pots and pans. The boy went on to graduate from an industrial high school and, with his father, later managed a factory subcontracting work from a shipbuilder. He married and raised two children. His father, however, suffered from aftereffects of the radiation, and died in 1983. His mother passed away in 1991, with her son and family by her side. (Photo by Yamahata Yosuke, 10 August 1945.)

乳をふくませる母　爆心地より3.5km、道ノ尾駅前の臨時救護所で、傷の手当てを待つ間、生後4か月の次男に乳をふくませた。彼女は国民学校1年生の長男を被爆4日目に亡くし、この次男も8月21日に息を引き取った。（撮影／1945年8月10日・山端庸介）

Breastfeeding mother. This victim took the opportunity to breastfeed her second son, four months old, while waiting for treatment at the first-aid station in front of Michinoo Station, 3.5 kilometers from ground zero. She lost her eldest son, in his first year of elementary school, four days after the bomb. On 21 August this second son, too, breathed his last. (Photo by Yamahata Yosuke, 10 August 1945.)

さまよう兄弟　弟の方の顔は頭部の負傷による出血で、それも暑さでひからびている。もちろん顔を洗う余裕などないのである。長崎駅付近をさまよっていた。

兄は当時18歳、弟は7歳。8月9日、弟の化膿した足の傷の治療で長崎医科大学付属病院（爆心地より700m）に入院するため、16km離れた炭鉱の島・高島から船でやってきた。両親も一緒だった。弟に母が付き添って治療室に入った時、原爆が炸裂した。両親と散りぢりになった2人は、長崎の親戚を求めてさまよっていた。兄が肩から下げているカバンには、国民学校1年生になったばかりの弟の勉強道具。長くなる入院のために弟を思ってもってきた。被爆の混乱のなかでも手放さなかった。母は島に帰りついた日、弟は敗戦の翌日・8月16日に死亡した。兄は戦後、炭鉱で機械修理の仕事をしていたが、1981年、激しい頭痛と真っ黒な液を吐き54歳の命を失った。（撮影／1945年8月10日朝7時頃・山端庸介）

Brothers wandering aimlessly. The blood from the younger brother's head wound had dried in the heat. Most likely they could not stop to wash the wounds as they wandered in the area around Nagasaki Station.

The elder of the brothers was 18 at the time; the younger, only 7. They had arrived in Nagasaki with their parents that very day, travelling by ship from their home on the island of Takashima, a mining community 16 kilometers away. The younger brother was to enter the Nagasaki Medical College Hospital (700 meters from ground zero) for treatment for an infected leg injury. He was in an examination room with his mother when the bomb was dropped. The boys were separated from their parents in the ensuing chaos and later wandered in search of their Nagasaki relatives. In the bag shouldered by the elder brother is schoolwork that his younger brother, a newly matriculated first grader, would have needed to keep up during the anticipated long stay in the hospital. Even in the confusion following the bombing they did not let this bag out of their sight. The mother died on the day she returned to her home island; the younger brother on 16 August, the day after Japan's surrender. The elder brother later worked doing maintenance on mining equipment. He suffered from migraine headaches and died in 1981 at the age of 54, vomiting a pitch-black liquid. (Photo by Yamahata Yosuke, 10 August 1945, approximately 7 a.m.)

防空壕からカメラにほほえむ少女　爆心地より2.5km、中町天主堂がかすかに見える。

　悲惨な光景が続く原爆写真のなかで、救いのようなこの1枚は、1952年9月29日号の雑誌『ライフ』に「ラッキーガール」として掲載されたが、現実は被爆者であったが故の悲劇を生き、放射能による白血病が原因で51歳の生涯を終えたのだった。

　被爆時、彼女は18歳。長崎の姉夫婦を頼って故郷・熊本を離れ、国鉄の女性車掌として働いていた。被爆1週後、同じ職場の男性と結婚。4児をもうけるが、被爆15年目に白血病を発症。被爆時の精神的衝撃、病のおびえから逃れようと多量の飲酒にのめり込むようになり、24年の結婚生活にピリオドを打つ。入退院を繰り返していたが、晩年は手足も不自由になり、言語障害も現れたという。（撮影／1945年8月10日朝・山端庸介）

Girl in a bomb shelter smiles for the camera. The site is 2.5 kilometers from ground zero, and the Nakamachi Cathedral is vaguely visible in the background.

This photograph comes as a welcome relief in the long series of pictures depicting the devastation of Nagasaki after the atomic bombing. It originally appeared in *Life* magazine on 29 September 1952. Though titled "Lucky Girl," the reality is far different: leukemia caused by radiation exposure led to her death at the age of 51, making this woman's life another tragedy caused by the atomic bomb.

She was eighteen years old at the time of the bombing. Having left her hometown of Kumamoto, she was living with her married elder sister in Nagasaki and working as a conductor for the National Railways. Just one week after the bombing she married a colleague at the railway. They were blessed with four children but, fifteen years after the bomb dropped, she was struck with leukemia. Anxiety over this illness and the lingering psychological stress from the atomic bombing pushed her towards alcoholism, and her twenty-four year marriage came to an end. In and out of hospitals, she was left incapacitated and largely unable to speak in her final years. (Photo by Yamahata Yosuke, 10 August 1945, morning.)

火葬　被爆後1か月がたっても、市内各所の空き地で火葬が行なわれていた。(撮影／1945年8月下旬・松本栄一)

Cremation.　Even a month after the bombing, bodies were still being cremated in vacant lots across the city.　(Photo by Matsumoto Eiichi, late August 1945.)

祈り　被爆1年後の浦上天主堂で。原爆によって浦上信徒1万2,000人のうち7割を超える8,500人余りが亡くなった。生き残った信徒が中心になって、瓦礫を片付け、再建のための煉瓦を積み上げた。一応の完成を見たのは、14年後、1959年であった。(撮影／1946年・山端庸介)

Prayer.　This photo was taken a year after the bombing at the Urakami Cathedral, which lost approximately 70% of its parishioners (8,500 fatalities among 12,000 members) to the bomb.　The survivors assisted in clearing the rubble and restacking the bricks, but even the initial restoration was not completed until 1959, fourteen years after the bombing. (Photo by Yamahata Yosuke, 1946.)

53

悪魔の申し子を、だれが――

井上ひさし

　毎年、8月が近づくと、「だれがヒロシマとナガサキに原子爆弾を落としたのか」という思いにとらわれてしまいます。もちろん、どなたに聞いても同じ答えが返ってきます。「そんなの決まってら、アメリカ合衆国じゃないか」

　たしかにその通り、原爆を投下したのはアメリカ合衆国の戦争指導者層です。これはまちがいない。ひどいやつらです。許せない。

　けれども、投下までの事実の経過を正確かつ克明に辿って行くと、びっくりすることに、共犯者が大勢いたのです。

　当時の大日本帝国の戦争指導者層のうち、宮廷グループと称される人たちは、昭和20（1945）年の初めにはすでに和平への道を探りはじめていました。事実、彼等はソ連を通して和平交渉を進めようとしていました。

　ただし、彼等には、どうしても譲れない条件があった。国体の維持です。天皇の身分についての保証です。明治憲法第一条の「大日本帝国ハ萬世一系ノ天皇之ヲ統治ス」を認めさせる。他のことなら受け入れるが、これだけは譲れない。

　もちろん、日本の宮廷グループが戦争を終わらせたがっているということは、ソ連を通じてアメリカの指導者層の耳に入っています。

　その年の7月17日、米、英、ソの首脳による会談が、ドイツのポツダムで開かれますが、じつはその前日、アメリカのニューメキシコ州のアラモゴードの砂漠で核実験が成功していた……。

　これで共犯者探しの材料がそろいました。さて、ここからが本論です。

　会談の期間中の7月26日、会談の決議が日本に通告されます。これが例のポツダム宣言です。連合国側は、ソ連を通して、日本の宮廷グループによる和平の模索とその条件を知っている。ですから、もしも本気で戦争を終結させたいのなら、宣言の中に、天皇の身分を保証する文言が書き込んであってもよさそうなものですが、そのことについてはなにも書かれていなかった。なぜでしょうか。

　原爆の悪魔的な威力を武器に、大戦後の世界の経営を有利に進めようとしていたアメリカのトルーマン大統領がイギリスのチャーチル首相と相談して、天皇の身分の保証についてはふれずにおいたのです。つまり彼等は、もうしばらく戦争をつづけたかった。もっと言えば、日本に原爆を落としたかったのです。その威力をスターリンに見せつけて、ソ連を牽制しようとしたわけです。

　スターリンはスターリンで、日本がこの最後通牒を受け入れないよう祈っていました。その年4月のヤルタ会談の密約で、もしも日本が連合国側からの最後通牒を拒否するようなら、ソ連も日本に宣戦布告をすると決まっていたからです。参戦して日本を叩き、日本に勝つ。そして戦果の分け前にあずかろうという計算です。ですからスターリンも、天皇の身分の保証を書き込まないことに賛成した。やはりソ連も戦さをつづけたかったわけです。

　さて、日本政府はどうしたか。天皇の身分についての保証が書かれていないことにこだわって、この宣言を黙殺してしまった。そのことによって、アメリカには原爆を投下する理由ができたのです。

　こうして連合国側の戦争指導者層が、そろいもそろってみな共犯者たちだということがわかりました。そればかりでなく、「帝国臣民はみなわが赤子（せきし）」と唱えていた日本の戦争指導者層もその仲間だったことがわかった。あの人たちがほんとうに大事にしていたのは、わたしたち赤子ではなかった。ということは、大日本帝国も含めて世界中の戦争指導者層が、寄ってたかってヒロシマとナガサキにあの悪魔の申し子を投下したのではないか。

　……こう考えがまとまってからは、わたしは指導者というものを一切、信じないことにしました。目を皿のようにして彼等の一挙手一投足を見張っているようにしたい。そして彼等がいったいなにをやったか、それを見定めたいと願っているのです。(1998年5月「the座」37号より改題)

いのうえ・ひさし　1934年、山形県生まれ。劇作家・小説家。1971年、戯曲『道元の冒険』で芸術選奨新人賞、翌年岸田戯曲賞、小説『手鎖心中』で直木賞受賞。1981年、小説『吉里吉里人』で日本SF大賞、翌年読売文学賞。1986年、小説『腹鼓記』『不忠臣蔵』で吉川英治文学賞。1981年、こまつ座を結成、原爆をテーマに『父と暮らせば』、『紙屋町さくらホテル』など多くの戯曲を書く。著書にエッセイ『にほん語観察ノート』（中央公論新社）など多数。

Who Unleashed Satan's Handiwork?   Inoue Hisashi

Every year as August approaches I find myself obsessed with the question "Who dropped the atomic bombs on Hiroshima and Nagasaki?" Anyone I ask, of course, gives me the same answer: "It was, obviously, the United States."

That is certainly true: the atomic bombs were dropped on the orders of the leaders of the United States. Of that there is no doubt, and what these detestable men did is unforgivable.

Still, carefully tracing the steps that led up to the bombings is a shocking enterprise, for it reveals a large cast of co-conspirators.

Among the military leaders of the Japanese empire at the time, the group known as the Imperial Court Faction was already exploring the road to peace in early 1945. They were working through the Soviet Union to negotiate an end to the war. However, there existed a certain condition on which they would not compromise: they insisted on the preservation of the *kokutai*, the basic structure of the Japanese state, including a guarantee that the status of the Emperor would be secure. While they were willing to negotiate on other issues, the Imperial Family's right to sovereignty over the empire as stated in Article One of the Meiji Constitution was to remain sacred. This desire on the part of the Imperial Court Faction to end the war was made known to the leaders of the United States through the Soviet Union.

Meanwhile, the heads of state from America, England, and the Soviet Union opened a conference in Potsdam, Germany, on 17 July 1945, the very day after the Americans had successfully tested a nuclear weapon in the desert outside Alamagordo, New Mexico.

With this the cast of co-conspirators is in place, and I can proceed to my main point.

The resolutions passed at the conference, the famous Potsdam Declaration, were conveyed to Japan on 26 July 1945, while the talks were ongoing. At the time, the Allied Forces had already been notified by the Soviet Union of the Imperial Court Faction's desire to end the war as well as their condition for surrender. Had the Allies truly wanted peace, they could have included in their resolutions a guarantee of the Emperor's status, but not a word to this effect was mentioned. Why?

U.S. President Truman had decided to deploy the satanic power of the atomic bomb to further his agenda for the postwar world and, in consultation with Churchill of Great Britain, he had intentionally omitted mention of the fate of the Emperor. Simply put, both men wanted the war to continue a little longer and both wanted to drop the atomic bomb on Japan because they hoped that, by demonstrating its power to Stalin, they would be better able to contain the Soviet Union.

Stalin had his own reasons for wanting the war to continue, and he too hoped Japan would not accept this final ultimatum. At the Yalta Conference of April 1945 it had been decided that should Japan reject the final proposition from the Allied Forces, the Soviet Union would declare war on Japan. With their participation Japan would soon capitulate and, as a member of the victorious forces, the Soviet Union would share in the spoils of war. These were reasons enough for Stalin to support the omission of any guarantee of the Emperor's continued sovereignty.

How did the Japanese government respond? They ignored the proposal, refusing to even consider it because it did not meet their condition concerning the Emperor. At this point the United States had its excuse for dropping the atomic bomb.

From this progression of events it is clear that every leader of the Allied Forces was a co-conspirator in the deployment of nuclear weapons. It is also clear that the military leaders of Japan aided and abetted this effort. While they mouthed the phrase "all imperial subjects are our children," quite clearly their devotion was directed elsewhere. It was the wartime leaders of all nations, including those of the Japanese Empire, that unleashed Satan's handiwork on Hiroshima and Nagasaki.

Once I reached this conclusion, I decided never again to trust any leader. I intend to keep my eyes wide open, watching every move that they make. I am determined to monitor them so that nothing will go unnoticed.

(Excerpts from an article originally published in *The Za*, no. 37, May 1998.)

Inoue Hisashi. Born in Yamagata Prefecture in 1934, Inoue is an award-winning playwright and novelist. His play "Dogen no boken" (The adventures of the monk Dogen, 1971) won both the Ministry of Education's Recommended Reading Newcomer Award and, in 1972, the Kishida Prize for playwrights. That same year his novel *Tegusari shinju* (Handcuffed double suicide) was awarded the Naoki Prize. In 1981 his *Kirikirijin* (The Kirikirians) won the Japan Science Fiction Award and, the following year, the Yomiuri Literary Prize. His 1986 novels *Haratsuzumiki* (*The Badger's Tummy Drum*) and *Fuchushingura* (Treasury of unfaithful retainers) earned him the Yoshikawa Prize. He formed the Komatsu Theater Group in 1981, and has written many plays for them, including *Chichi to kuraseba* (Living with father, 1995), which deals with the atomic bombs, and *Kamiya-cho Sakura Hotel* (The Cherry Blossom Hotel in the Kamiya District.) He also has numerous essay collections, such as *Nihongo kansatsu note* (Field notes on the Japanese language), to his name.

福田須磨子

花こそは心のいこい

人々よ　つどい来たりて
花のたね　いざ蒔かん。
一粒のたねの生命(いのち)は
わかき芽をふき　美しき花とはならん。
そはやがて　散りて行くとも
いつの日か　あゝ　いつの日か
失なわれし　わが故郷を
かぐわしき　花園とせん。

人々よ　つどい来たりて
花の唄　いざ歌わん
花こそは　心のいこい。
生き難き世の　美しき虹のかけ橋。
そはやがて　夢とつながり
いつの日か　あゝ　いつの日か
手を組みし　遠き国をも
かぐわしく　埋めつくさん。

Flowers Are a Comfort to the Soul Fukuda Sumako

People, come and gather 'round.
Let us sow seeds, the seeds of flowers.
The life within a single seed
Sprouts first a bud, then turns into a beautiful flower.
They will, in time, scatter to the wind,
But someday, yes, someday,
We will make the hometown that we lost
A fragrant garden full of flowers.

People, come and gather 'round.
Let us sing songs, the songs of flowers.
Flowers are a comfort to the soul.
They are a beautiful rainbow bridging out of this hostile world.
They will, in time, nurture dreams,
And someday, yes, someday,
We will join hands with even distant lands
Filling all with the fragrance of dreams.

ふくだ・すまこ（1922〜1974）長崎市生まれ。詩人。被爆で受けた肉体の苦痛と心の亀裂をうたった『詩集　原子野』を刊行。反核の直接行動にも参加。放射能の後遺症とたたかいながら、被爆者の生活記録『われなお生きてあり』を書く。

Fukuda Sumako (1922~1974). This poet, native to Nagasaki, is the author of *Shishu: Genshiya* (Poems of the atomic wilderness), an anthology of poems dealing with the physical suffering and psychological trauma of the a-bomb victims. She was also active in the anti-nuclear movement. While battling the effects of radiation poisoning herself, she chronicled the lives of other atomic bomb victims. These writings were published as *Ware nao ikite ari* (Still we live).

表現された「地獄」の諸相

The Varied Representations of "Hell"

「原爆の図」第1部－「幽霊」部分図
全体図＝180.0×720.0㎝（4曲1双の
屏風）1950年
丸木位里・丸木俊
「……着物は燃え落ち、…皮膚はぼろ
のようにたれさがった。手をなかばあ
げて、それは幽霊の行列」（図に添え
られた画家の文より）
（所蔵／原爆の図丸木美術館）

"Hiroshima Panels," section of
painting 1, "Ghost."
Total size: 180.0 x 720.0 cm (four
section folding screen). 1950.
Maruki Iri and Maruki Toshi.
"... their kimonos were burned off
their bodies and their skin dangled
from their limbs. Arms raised, this
parade of ghosts marched on."
(Excerpt from the artists' text
accompanying the paintings.)
(Maruki Gallery for The Hiroshima
Panels.)

「原爆の図」第2部－「火」部分図
全体図＝180.0×720.0㎝（4曲1双の
屏風）1950年
丸木位里・丸木俊
「……めらめらと燃えあがり、広漠た
る廃墟の静寂を破って、ごうごうと燃
えていったのでありました」
（所蔵／原爆の図丸木美術館）

"Hiroshima Panels," section of
painting 2, "Fire."
Total size: 180.0 x 720.0 cm (four
section folding screen). 1950.
Maruki Iri and Maruki Toshi.
". . . flames climbed ever higher,
shattering the quiet of the vast
stretch of ruins, engulfing all in a wild
inferno."
(Maruki Gallery for The Hiroshima
Panels.)

　広島で、あるいは長崎で未だかつて経験したことのない
「破壊」と「殺戮」に遭遇し生き残った人びとは、「怒り」や
「悲しみ」のなかで自分が経験したことの意味を考え、それ
を人びとに伝えようとした。「このことを書き残さなければ
ならない」と心に誓い『夏の花』3部作を書いた原民喜をは
じめ、戦後占領軍がしいたプレス・コード（検閲）の網の目
をくぐって、「原爆文学」といわれる一連の作品を書き残し
た人びとに、それは代表される。彼らは、原爆＝核の非人間
性と大規模な環境破壊に「異議申し立て」を行なった。

　そして、この原爆＝核を表現する意思は、文学者にとどま
らず、さまざまなジャンルの表現者から「素人」の市民にま
でおよんでいった。世界中の誰よりも先に原爆の犠牲となり、
生き残った被爆者や、想像力を武器にこの世界のあり様と対
峙してきた人びとは、このような悲惨な出来事が二度とこの
地球上で起こって欲しくないとの願いを込めて、未曾有の
「破壊」と「殺戮」への表現に向かっていったのである。

　そして、「記録」を代表するのが本書に収めた被爆直後に
撮られた写真の数々であるとするならば、「表現」を代表す
るのが「原爆文学」であり、丸木位里（1901～1995）・俊（1912～
2000）夫妻による「原爆の図」（1950～1982年制作）をはじめと
する、市民が描いた作品をも含めた絵画や版画作品であった。
「原爆の図」は、第1部「幽霊」に始まり「火」「水」「虹」
「少年少女」「原子野」「竹やぶ」「救出」「焼津」「署名」「母
子像」「とうろう流し」「米兵捕虜の死」「からす」「長崎」と
全15部、さまざまな角度から原爆の被害を描いたものであ
る。

　「原爆の図」は、専門的な表現者による「反核」を底意に
もった思想によって描きだされたものであるが、広島や長崎
の市民による絵画表現は、脳裏を去らない惨劇を今一度紙の
上に再現することで、原爆＝核の悲惨・非人間性を訴えるリ
アルな（素朴な）表現と言えるだろう。川を流れる死体の群
れ、死んだ母子、斃れた馬、焼かれる死体、これらは「ヒロ
シマ・ナガサキ」が紛れもなく「地獄」であったことを、如
実に表していた。ここからは、「ノーモア・ヒロシマ」「ノー
モア・ナガサキ」の声が聞こえてくる。

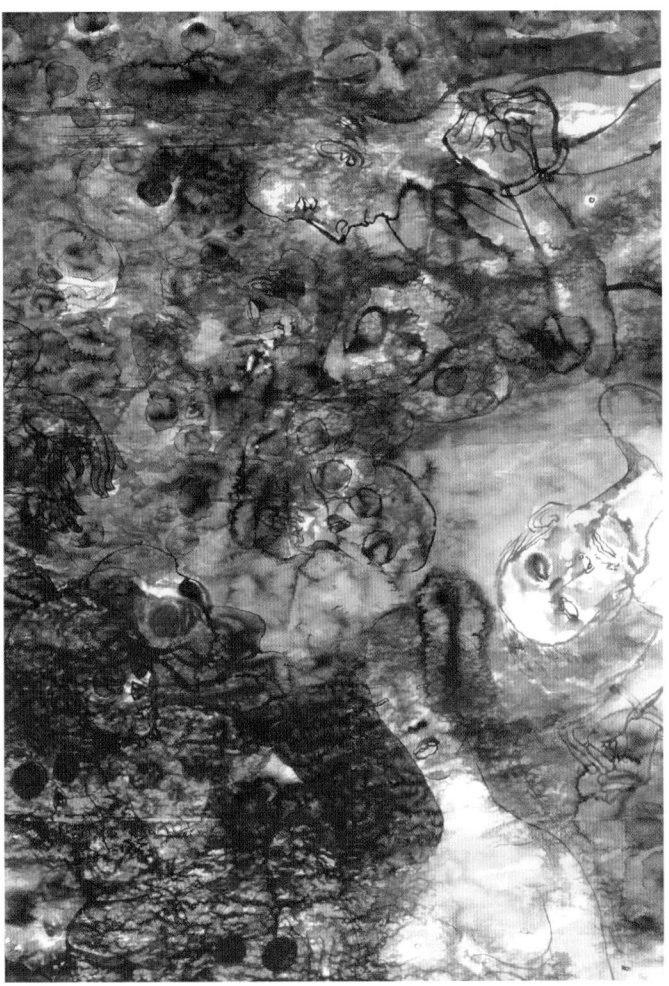

「原爆の図」第13部－「米軍捕虜の死」
部分図
全体図＝180.0×720.0㎝（4曲1双の
屏風）1971年
丸木位里・丸木俊
「…あなたの原爆であなたのお国の若
者も23人死んだのです。…女の捕虜
もいたという」
（所蔵／原爆の図丸木美術館）

"Hiroshima Panels," section of
painting 13, "Death of American
Prisoners-of-War."
Total size: 180.0 x 720.0 cm (four
section folding screen). 1971.
Maruki Iri and Maruki Toshi.
". . . and by an atomic bomb of your
own making 23 young people of your
own country perished. . . . Some say
there were women prisoners among
them."
(Maruki Gallery for The Hiroshima
Panels.)

After their encounter with the unprecedented destruction and carnage brought by the atomic bombing of Hiroshima and Nagasaki, those who survived pondered in their anger and grief the meaning of what they had experienced and they sought to relate their thoughts to others. Determined to leave behind a record of their experience, writers took advantage of loopholes in the Occupation Forces' Press Code, the means by which censorship was enforced. Beginning with *Summer Flowers*, a trilogy by Hara Tamiki, they left behind works now known as "a-bomb literature." It was their way of voicing their objection to the inhumanity and colossal environmental damage wreaked by the atomic bomb.

Writers were not the only ones driven by a desire to express their thoughts on the bomb–artists working in a wide variety of media as well as ordinary citizens did much the same. In hopes of preventing a repetition of this horrendous event, surviving victims of the world's first atomic bombs were joined by others, and together they unleashed the power of their imaginations on a world they would not tolerate. They struggled to forge a means of representing the unprecedented destruction and carnage of Hiroshima and Nagasaki.

If the many photographs taken immediately after the atomic bombings (some of which are included here) constitute a "record"of the event, then a-bomb literature and the paintings and prints dealing with the bombings, some done by ordinary citizens, comprise "representations" of the tragedy. First among the visual artists were Maruki Iri (1901~ 1995) and his wife Toshi (1912~2000). Their "Hiroshima Panels" (1950~ 82) is a series of fifteen paintings depicting the atomic bombing from a wide variety of perspectives. Included in this series are works titled "Ghost," "Fire," "Water," "Rainbow," "Boys and Girls," "Atomic Desert," "Bamboo Thicket," "Rescue," "Yaizu," "Petition," "Mother and Child," "Floating Lanterns," "Death of American Prisoners of War," "Crows," and "Nagasaki."

In addition to the "Hiroshima Panels," which were produced by professional artists based on their anti-nuclear convictions, we also have images created by the average citizens of Hiroshima and Nagasaki. There is something "raw," something intensely real, about these pictures, and they haunt the viewer with their representations of the horror and inhumanity of the atomic bomb. Mounds of corpses floating down the river, a dead mother and child, a lifeless horse, scorched human remains–these pictures depict Hiroshima and Nagasaki as indeed a "hell" upon earth. They call out to us–"No more Hiroshima, Nagasaki."

1945年8月6日、私立修道中学3年生（15歳）の平山郁夫さんは、動員された陸軍兵器補給廠で被爆。すべてを焼きつくす炎、無数の死体、死に瀕した被爆者の姿を目撃し、自身も原爆に蝕まれる数年を過ごした。

その時から34年目、不死鳥のように再生した広島に触発され、ようやく原爆を描く確信を得る。炎に巻かれながら人びとに「生きよ！」と叫ぶ憤怒の不動明王を構想することで、平山さんの唯一の「原爆図」は成った。

On 6 August 1945, Mr. Hirayama, fifteen years old and a third-year student at Shudo Middle School, was working as a mobilized student in the army ammunition depot when the bomb was dropped. He saw with his own eyes the all-engulfing flames, the countless corpses, and the victims on the verge of death; he himself suffered for some years from the effects of the bomb.

It was only in the 34th year after the bomb that, having seen Hiroshima rise like a phoenix from the ashes, he finally felt he could address the atomic bomb in his art. Mr. Hirayama's single a-bomb work shows an enraged Fudo the Immovable, a Buddhist guardian deity, calling out to the people wrapped in flames below. His message: "Live!"

広島生変図
紙本彩色六曲屏風
171.0×364.0㎝　1979年
平山郁夫（1930〜）
広島県出身　日本美術院理事長　東京
芸術大学学長　文化勲章受章
（所蔵／広島県立美術館）

Hiroshima: The Cataclysm.
Six section folding screen, color on paper.
Total size: 171.0 x 364.0 cm. 1979.
 Hirayama Ikuo (1930 ~). Native of Hiroshima, Director of the Japan Fine Arts Institute, President of Tokyo National University of Fine Arts and Music.
(Hiroshima Prefectural Art Museum.)

霊歌「ヒロシマ」
29.0×36.4㎝　1988年
秀島由己男（1934～）
熊本県出身　版画家
（所蔵／広島市現代美術館）

A Requiem for Hiroshima.
Total size: 29.0 x 36.4 cm.
1988.
Hideshima Yukio (1934 ~). Native of
Kumamoto, woodblock artist.
(Hiroshima City Museum of
Contemporary Art.)

国道２号線古江附近
黒い雨降る（八時三十五分頃）
（半身焼たゞれ頭髪半分はがれた
路傍の乙女は、もう動かない娘さん）

被爆直後から広島市街地は大火災となり、猛烈な火事嵐・竜巻が発生した。20〜30分もすると、黒く汚れた大粒の雨が降った。巻き上げられた泥やスス・チリなどによる汚れと、強い放射能を含んでいた。

　水を求めていた人びとは、水たまりに群がったり、口を開けて降る雨を飲んだが、後に深刻な放射能障害をもたらす原因となった。

Immediately after the bombing all the streets of Hiroshima were in flames. Intense firestorms burst out everywhere, and tornadoes ripped through the city. Twenty or thirty minutes later large drops of black rain fell, dirtied by the mud, dust, and smoke raised by the bomb and filled with radiation.

　Throngs of people seeking water gathered around puddles or opened their mouths to drink the falling rain. These actions were to cause serious radiation poisoning in the days to come.

黒い雨降る
伊藤貫一
「国道2号線古江付近
黒い雨降る（8時35分頃）
（半身焼けただれ、頭髪半分はがれた娘さん。
路傍の乙女は、もう動かない）」
（提供／広島平和記念資料館）

Black Rain.
Ito Kanichi.
"National Highway 2 in the vicinity of Furue.
Black rain falls (approximately 8:35 a.m.)
(A young woman with burned skin dangling from one side of her body. One side of her head, too, is left bald. The young woman lying on the road was to move no more.)"
(Provided courtesy of Hiroshima Peace Memorial Museum.)

母と子
松添博（1930～）
長崎市生まれ。長崎美術協会理事、長崎原爆継承部会会員（語り部）、元長崎原爆被害者療養センター所長。1985年、1か月半にわたりアメリカ・テキサス大学で原爆絵画を含む日本画展を開催、原爆の悲惨を訴える。
（所蔵／長崎原爆資料館）

Mother and Child.
Matsuzoe Hiroshi (1930 ~).
Native of Nagasaki, Director of the Nagasaki Association for the Arts, Member of the Nagasaki Society.of the Atomic Bomb Legacy (kataribe narrator), former Director of the Nagasaki Atomic Bomb Victim Medical Center. In 1985 Matsuzoe spent a month and a half at the University of Texas, U.S.A., where he related the horrors of the atomic bombs as part of a Japanese art exhibit that included paintings of the bombings.
(Nagasaki Atomic Bomb Museum.)

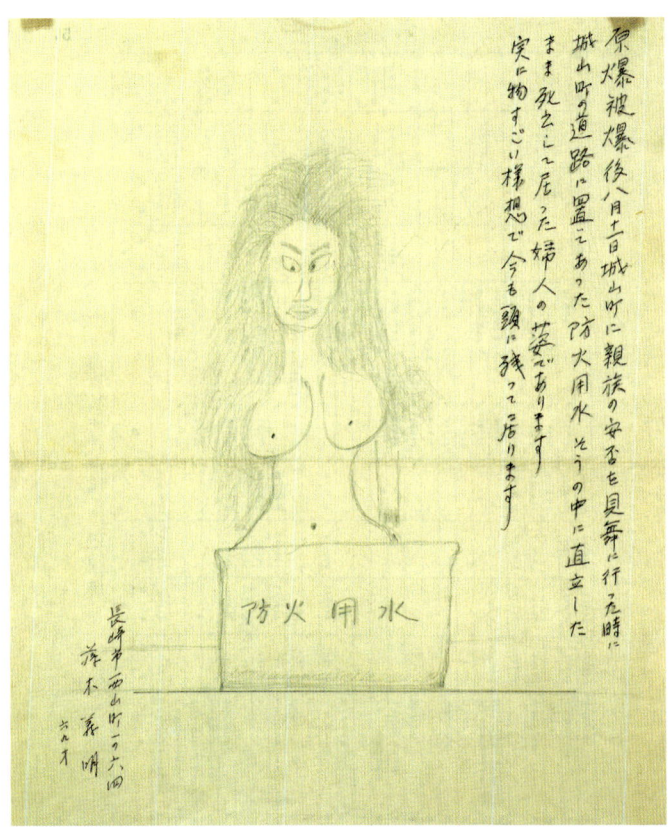

原爆被爆後八月十一日城山町に親族の安否を見舞いに行った時に城山町の道路に置てあった防火用水そうの中に直立したまま死亡した婦人の姿であります実に物すごい様相で今も頭に残って居ります

直立したまま死ぬ女性
藤本義明
「原爆被爆後8月11日、城山町に親族の安否を見舞いに行った時に、城山町の道路に置いてあった防火用水槽の中に、直立したまま死亡しておった婦人の姿であります。実に物すごい様相で、今も頭に残っております」

Standing in Death.
Fujimoto Yoshiaki.
"On my way to check on the fate of relatives in Shiroyama-cho, Nagasaki, on 11 August, just two days after the bombing, I came across the body of a woman who had died standing up in a water tank that had been placed by the side of the road for fighting fires. It was such a horrific sight that it haunts me still."

浦上駅付近で爆死した馬と女性の頭皮
島田鶴彦

Near Urakami Station: Dead Horse and the Hair of a Woman Who was Killed in the Blast.
Shimada Tsuruhiko.

傷痕から
75.5×60.5cm　1966年
上野誠（1909～1980）
長野市生まれ。東京・鹿児島・岐阜で
小・中学校の美術教師。戦後、日本美
術会・日本版画協会会員。1961年、
長崎を訪れ、版画家として原爆に取り
組み、日本および世界各地で個展を開
催、反核・平和を訴えた。

Wounds.
75.5 x 60.5 cm. 1966.
Ueno Makoto (1909 ~ 1980). A native
of Nagano city, Ueno worked as an art
instructor in elementary and middle
schools in Tokyo, Kagoshima and
Gifu. After the war he was a member
of the Japan Association of the Fine
Arts and the Japan Print Association.
After visiting Nagasaki in 1961, Ueno
began to address the issue of the
atomic bomb in his work as a
woodblock print artist. Later, through
one-man exhibits in Japan and various
locations all over the world, he made
his case against nuclear weapons and
issued an appeal for peace.

長崎の像
58.0×45.0cm　1963年
上野誠

A Portrait of Nagasaki.
58.0 x 45.0 cm. 1963.
Ueno Makoto.

聖像
16.0×28.0㎝　1974年
小崎侃（1942〜）
長崎在住の版画家。熊本市に生まれ長崎に育つ。現代美術家協会新人賞、版画グランプリなどを受賞、数多くの国内・国際展に出品。反核・平和を訴える多くの作品を制作する。

Sacred Statues.
16.0 x 28.0 cm. 1974.
Kozaki Kan (1942 ~).
Born in Kumamoto City and raised in Nagasaki, Kozaki now works as a woodblock print artist in Nagasaki. Kozaki, who has won both the Modern Art Association's New Artist Award and the Woodblock Print Grand Prix, exhibits his work in numerous venues both in Japan and abroad. Many of his works express an anti-nuclear orientation and a desire for peace.

3人の子
30.0×23.0㎝　1983〜1987年
小崎侃
長崎の俳人・松尾あつゆき（1904〜1983）は、家族4人の命を奪った原爆の悲惨を『原爆句抄』200句に詠んだが、小崎さんはその全ての句を題材に木版画連作「合掌」を制作した。この作品はそのなかの1点。
「ここに三人の子を眠らせて　若葉 雲湧くごとし──あつゆき」

Three Children.
30.0 x 23.0 cm. 1983 ~ 1987.
Kozaki Kan.
This print is one of 200 in Kozaki's *Gassho* (Hands in prayer), a series accompanying *Genbaku kusho* (A-bomb haiku), a poetry collection in which Matsuo Atsuyuki (1904 ~1983) writes of his grief at having lost four family members to the bomb. The poem here reads: "Here lie three children, Springing forth like young leaves, like clouds. Atsuyuki."

ダビ——悲しい別れ
74.0×92.0cm　1985年
松添博（1930〜）
（所蔵／長崎原爆資料館）

Farewell: The Simplest of Rites for
the Dead.
74.0 x 92.0 cm. 1985.
Matsuzoe Hiroshi (1930~).
(Nagasaki Atomic Bomb Museum.)

コレガ人間ナノデス　　　　原　民喜

コレガ人間ナノデス
原子爆弾ニ依ル変化ヲゴラン下サイ
肉体ガ恐ロシク膨脹シ
男モ女モスベテ一ツノ型ニカヘル
オオ　ソノ真黒焦ゲノ滅茶苦茶ノ
爛レタ顔ノムクンダ唇カラ洩レテ来ル声ハ
「助ケテ下サイ」
ト　カ細イ　静カナ言葉
コレガ　コレガ人間ナノデス
人間ノ顔ナノデス

This Is A Human Being   Hara Tamiki

Yes, this is a human being.
Please look carefully at the changes wrought by the atomic bomb.
The body is so grotesquely bloated that
Anything male or female about it has been erased.
From the swollen lips on the festering face, ravaged and charred black,
Oozes a quiet, wavering voice:
"Help me, please."
This, yes, this is a human being.
Yes, this is the face of a human being.

はら・たみき （1905〜1951）広島市生まれ。小説家・詩人。爆心地より1.4kmの兄宅で被爆。その体験をもとにした『夏の花』、詩集に『原民喜詩集』がある。朝鮮戦争の勃発に、再び原爆が使われるかもしれないという戦争の恐怖を抱き、鉄道自殺。

Hara Tamiki (1905 ~ 1951).
Hara, a novelist and poet, was in his elder brother's home 1.4 kilometers from ground zero when the bomb was dropped on his native Hiroshima. He recorded his experiences in the trilogy titled *Summer Flowers*. He has also published poetry, including *Hara Tamiki shishu* (An anthology of poems by Hara Tamiki). Tortured by fears that the Korean War would lead to another use of nuclear weapons, Hara committed suicide by leaping in front of a train.

髪の抜けることを気にしながら死んだ
弟
1985年
山下蘇朴（1917〜）
広島県生まれ。被爆時、建物疎開の作
業に動員された弟（当時18歳）を8月
末に原爆症で亡くす。戦後、水墨画に
取り組み、画集『閃光の軌跡』を出版、
各国首脳、平和団体に寄贈し、核兵器
の廃絶を訴えた。

Younger Brother, Who Died
Worried About Having Lost His Hair.
1985.
Yamashita Masato (1917 ~).
A native of Hiroshima, Yamashita lost
his younger brother to atomic bomb
disease at the end of August 1945.
The brother, 18 years old at the time
of the bombing, had been mobilized to
create fire blocks by dismantling
homes in the city. After the war
Yamashita concentrated on ink
paintings, some of which he later
published as *Senko no kiseki* (Traces
of the flash). As part of his campaign
to abolish nuclear weapons, he
donated copies of this work to heads
of state and organizations dedicated to
peace.

目玉の飛び出した少年
1985年
山下蘇朴
「くわいのような少年の目玉が、胸の
前にぶらさがっていた」（弟の話より）

Boy Whose Eyes Burst from their
Sockets.
1985.
Yamashita Masato.
"The young boy's eyeballs hung
down as low as his chest, like some
turnip." (As related by his younger
brother.)

原爆遺品

遺体の確認もなく遺品を残すことさえなく、死亡した人は多い。もの言わぬ証言者として、残された遺品は、広島平和記念資料館に1万8,000点が、長崎原爆資料館に約1万点が保管されている。

Many were the bodies that were never identified, many were the dead who left nothing behind by which they could be remembered. Bearing silent witness to the bombings, though, are about 18,000 articles held in the Hiroshima Peace Memorial Museum and about 10,000 articles in the collection at the Nagasaki International Culture Hall.

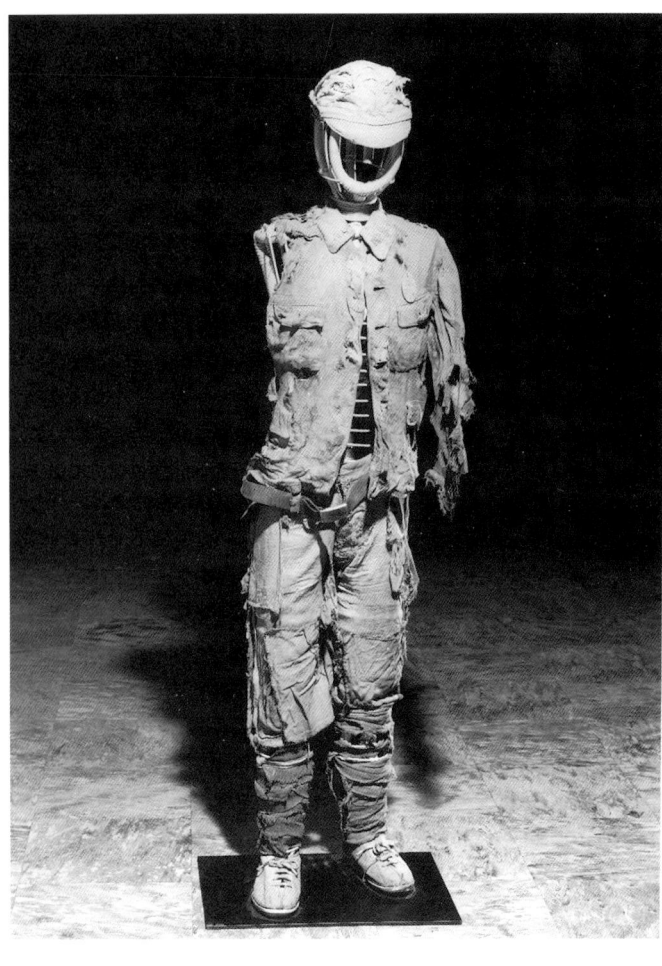

3人の中学生の衣服　爆心地より900mの小網町の建物疎開に動員されていた市立中学生353人は、その大半が死亡した。これは3人の生徒が身につけていた遺品を1体の人形としたもの。（所蔵／広島平和記念資料館＝津田蔵吉・福岡重春・上田キヨ寄贈　撮影／土田ヒロミ）

Uniforms of Three Middle School Students. From middle schools in the city 353 students had been mobilized and sent to Koami-cho, 900 meters from ground zero, to dismantle buildings in the creation of firebreaks. A majority of them died in the bombing. Pieces of the uniforms worn by three of them are used to partially clothe this mannequin. (Property of the Hiroshima Peace Memorial Museum; photo by Tsuchida Hiromi.)

三輪車　爆心地より1.5km、東白島町で三輪車に乗って遊んでいた3歳の男の子は、被爆した夜に死亡。（写真提供／広島平和記念資料館＝鉄谷信男寄贈）

Tricycle. The three-year old boy playing on this tricycle in Higashi Hakushima-cho, 1.5 kilometers from ground zero, died the night after the bombing. (Provided courtesy of Hiroshima Peace Memorial Museum.)

72

下駄　広島市立第一高等女学校1年生は、動員学徒として爆心地より500mの材木町で建物疎開作業中に被爆し、全員が死亡。ある母親が3か月間、探しまわってこの下駄を発見した。すげた鼻緒で娘のものと確認。遺体は行方不明。（所蔵／広島平和記念資料館＝井上富子寄贈　撮影／土田ヒロミ）

Wooden Clog. The first-year students from the girls' high school were mobilized to create firebreaks in Zaimoku-cho, 500 meters from ground zero. The atomic bomb killed all of them. One mother searched the ruins for three months before finding this wooden clog. She recognized it as her daughter's by the cloth used for the toe-strap. Her daughter's body was never identified. (Property of Hiroshima Peace Memorial Museum; photo by Tsuchida Hiromi.)

半溶融した一升ビン（所蔵／広島平和記念資料館＝久保田精一・大津至寄贈　撮影／土田ヒロミ）

Partially Melted Glass Bottles. (Property of Hiroshima Peace Memorial Museum; photo by Tsuchida Hiromi.)

弁当箱　高等女学校の生徒のもの。ご飯とエンドウ豆は完全に炭化している。材木町で建物疎開作業中に被爆。崩壊した誓願寺の土壁の下から発見。遺体は行方不明。（所蔵／広島平和記念資料館＝渡辺茂寄贈　撮影／土田ヒロミ）

腕時計　1955年4月、平和記念館の東側にかかる元安川下流150mで発見された。被爆の時間を指している。持ち主不明。（所蔵／広島平和記念資料館＝中本ヒデノ寄贈　撮影／土田ヒロミ）

長崎の柱時計　爆心地より約1km、山王神社近くの民家にあったもの。爆風で損傷したが、針は爆発の瞬間11時2分を今も記憶している。（提供／長崎原爆資料館）

Lunch Box. This artifact belonged to one of the girls' high school students mobilized in Zaimoku-cho at the time the bomb dropped. Found at the foot of the earthen walls at the collapsed Seiganji Temple, the rice and snow peas inside have been completely carbonized. The remains of the owner were never identified. (Property of Hiroshima Peace Memorial Museum; photo by Tsuchida Hiromi.)

Wristwatch. This artifact was discovered in April 1955 in the Motoyasu River, which runs along the eastern side of Hiroshima Peace Memorial Museum. It was located 150 meters downstream. The hands of the watch have frozen at the moment the bomb exploded. (Property of Hiroshima Peace Memorial Museum; photo by Tsuchida Hiromi.)

Nagasaki Wall Clock. This clock hung in a residence near the Sanno Shrine, approximately 1 kilometer from ground zero. Though damaged by the blast, even today the clock indicates 11:02 a.m., the instant the bomb was detonated. (provided courtesy of Nagasaki Atomic Bomb Museum.)

広島・長崎に投下された原子爆弾の実物大模型　左が広島に投下されたウラニウム原爆（ニックネーム：リトルボーイ＝かわいい少年）、右が長崎に投下されたプルトニウム原爆（ファットマン＝太っちょ男）。アメリカ・ニューメキシコ州アルバクァーキーの原子博物館で。（撮影／豊崎博光）

Full scale models of the atomic bombs dropped on Hiroshima and Nagasaki. These models are on display in the National Atomic Museum in Albuquerque, New Mexico. On the left is "Little Boy," the uranium bomb dropped on Hiroshima; on the right is "Fat Man," the plutonium bomb that destroyed Nagasaki. (Photo by Toyosaki Hiromitsu.)

エノラ・ゲイの内部　日本時間の1945年8月6日午前1時45分、リトルボーイを搭載したＢ29エノラ・ゲイは、12名の乗員を乗せ、テニアン島（広島から東南2,740kmの洋上）を飛び立った。午前8時15分、エノラ・ゲイの爆撃手は原爆投下装置のスイッチを入れ、原爆は機体を離れ、落下していった。43秒後、地上580mで、人類史上最初に戦争で使用された原爆は炸裂した。写真はアメリカ・メリーランド州のスミソニアン航空博物館に展示されるエノラ・ゲイの原爆投下装置。（撮影／豊崎博光）

The Cockpit of the Enola Gay
On 6 August 1945, at 1:45 a.m. Japan time, the B29 Enola Gay left the island of Tinian, 2,740 km southeast of Hiroshima. It carried a crew of twelve and an atomic bomb. At 8:45 a.m. the bomber aboard pressed the release button, and the atomic bomb dropped out of the airplane. Forty-three seconds later, at an altitude of 580 meters, the bomb was detonated, the first wartime use of an atomic weapon in human history. This photograph shows the bomb release mechanism in the Enola Gay, which is exhibited in the Smithsonian National Air and Space Museum, U.S.A. (Photo by Toyosaki Hiromitsu.)

被爆を超えて、いま

■「原爆乙女」と呼ばれて…山岡ミチコさん（1930年生まれ）

文・写真／関邦久
（日本リアリズム写真集団広島支部）

27回の整形手術

山岡さんは広島市の旧制高等女学校から学徒動員で職場に向かう途中、爆心地から800mの路上で被爆した。全身大火傷をし、死線を彷徨ったが、奇跡的に命をとりとめた。しかし、思春期にある15歳の少女の顔はケロイドで盛り上がり、一時は自殺を考えるまで精神的に追いつめられたが、母親の愛に支えられ、生き抜く意志をもつようになった。10年後、アメリカのプロテスタント団体の働きかけで、25人の「原爆乙女」の1人としてケロイドの治療を受けるために渡米し、1年半の間に27回の整形手術を受けた。原爆を落とした国アメリカに行くことには抵抗があったが、ホームステイ先のアメリカ人や医師団の温かな人間性に触れ、アメリカという国家を

憎むのではなく、戦争そのものを憎むようになったという。

その後、1979年に原爆症の母を看取ってからは、ずっと1人で暮らしている。

被爆を証言する

1980年、山岡さんは人に勧められ、初めて原爆の体験を中学3年生に語った。これを契機に原爆の証言活動をすることで、被爆者としての存在理由を発見していくことになる。

「子どもたちに話していると、目を輝かし、時には涙ぐむ子どももいて、自分も元気をもらえるようで、生きがいを感じます。多い時には1日に数回の証言活動でも疲れを忘れます」と、情熱を燃やす。アメリカやマケドニアの高校生・大学生など、海外の学生たちも毎年広島を訪れ、山岡さんと交流をもつのを楽しみにしている。

川岸にある原爆瓦の記念碑の前では、60年前の痛切な記憶がよみがえる。「被爆直後、全身の火傷を鎮めるために満潮の川に飛び込もうと、友人と話しあいました。自分が躊躇している間に、友人は飛び込みアッという間に消えていきました。その友人の顔が浮かび、今も満潮の川を見るのも、近寄るのも怖い……」

命の証として

青春を原爆に奪われ、結婚もしないで被爆後の60年を生きてきた山岡さん。

「何よりも、この地球上から戦争をなくすことが大切。私たちが生きているこの日本が再び戦争をする国にならないように、みんなで考えていかなくては……」

山岡さんは取材する私との別れ際に、「広島・長崎の被爆者の悲劇を繰り返さないため、そしてこの世から核兵器をなくすために、命ある限り訴え続けていきたい」と語った。噛みしめるような静かな口調が私の胸に食い入った。

この本に自分のありようが掲載されるのも、自分が生きてきた証であるからと──。

2004年8月5日、原爆ドーム前の山岡ミチコさん。

Ms. Yamaoka Michiko, in front of the Atomic Bomb Dome in Hiroshima, 5 August 2004.

The Present: Life After the Bomb

Yamaoka Michiko, "Maiden of Hiroshima"

Text and photos by Seki Kunihisa, Hiroshima branch of the Japan Realist Photographers Association.

Twenty-Seven Sessions of Reconstructive Surgery

Ms. Yamaoka (1930–) was on her way from the old Hiroshima Girls' High School to the workplace she had been assigned as a mobilized student when the atomic bomb was dropped. She was 800 meters from ground zero, and suffered third-degree burns over her entire body. Though she teetered on the brink of death, by some miracle, she survived. To this fifteen year-old girl in the bloom of youth, however, the keloids which scarred her face pushed her into a psychological crisis that included thoughts of suicide. It was her mother's love that gave her the will to live.

Ten years later she was one of the twenty-five "Maidens of Hiroshima" invited by a Protestant organization to travel to the United States for treatment. In the course of a single year, she underwent twenty-seven sessions of reconstructive surgery. Ms. Yamaoka tells of how she had at first resisted the idea of travelling to America, the country that had dropped the atomic bomb. It was the warmth and concern of her homestay family and the team of doctors there, though, that taught her to hate not America, but rather the act of war itself.

After her return, she cared for her mother, sick with atomic bomb disease. Since her mother's death in 1979, she has lived alone.

Bearing Witness to the Atomic Bomb

At the encouragement of acquaintances, in 1980 Ms. Yamaoka first spoke of her experience of the atomic bomb. Her audience was a group of third-year middle school students. Through this encounter she discovered a new purpose in life for victims of the atomic bombings: bearing witness to the tragedy.

"When I'm talking to the children, their eyes sparkle with interest and sometimes a child's eyes well up with tears. I am energized by those eyes, and they make me realize that life is worth living. They make me forget the fatigue that comes with, at busy times, addressing numerous groups in a single day," says Ms. Yamaoka, brimming with enthusiasm. High school and university students from the United States and Macedonia visit Hiroshima each year, and they all look forward to the time they will spend with Ms. Yamaoka.

Her painful memories of sixty years ago come flooding back as she stands on the riverbank beside the memorial made of roofing tiles scorched by the bomb. "Right after the bombing, a friend and I talked about soothing the burns all over our bodies by jumping into the swollen river. I hesitated for a moment, and before I could react my friend had plunged into the river and disappeared. I can still see her face, and even now approaching or even seeing a high-running river fills me with fear . . ."

A Tribute to Life

The atomic bomb deprived Ms. Yamaoka of her youth, and she has refrained from marriage for the sixty years since.

"Nothing is more important than ridding this earth of warfare. We must all ponder ways to prevent Japan, our home, from ever again waging war. . ."

As I bid farewell to Ms. Yamaoka after our interview, through gritted teeth she quietly said, "As long as I live I will continue to speak out for the abolition of nuclear weapons from this earth, I will continue to bear witness so that the tragedies of Hiroshima and Nagasaki will not be repeated." I was deeply moved.

Inclusion of her story in this book is yet another testimony to what she has endured.

2004年8月5日、広島平和公園の川岸で中・高校生に体験を語る山岡さん。

Ms. Yamaoka, as she bears witness to the atomic bombings for middle and high school students by the river in the Hiroshima Peace Memorial Park, 5 August 2004.

文・写真／黒﨑晴生
（日本リアリズム写真集団長崎支部）

張り裂ける痛みを越えて

　長崎市に住む谷口さんは、自転車に乗って郵便配達中に住吉町（爆心地より1.8㎞）の路上で被爆した。16歳の郵便局員だった。

　背中は焼けただれ、左手の肩から手先まで皮膚が垂れ下がっていた。近くにあった三菱重工長崎兵器製作所のトンネル工場に避難し、そこで邪魔になる垂れ下った皮膚を切り取ってもらった。3日後、救助隊に助けだされ、臨時救護所を転々とした後、大村市の海軍病院に入院した。

　原子爆弾の熱線で背中全面を火傷したため、身動き一つできず、うつぶせのまま1年9か月を過ごした。そのせいで胸部と左頬、顎の筋肉が削げ落ちてしまった。

　1949年に退院し、職場に復帰したが、傷の痛みで休むことが多く、治療入院が続いた。

　1956年、「長崎原爆青年乙女の会」の結成に参加、その年に開催された原水爆禁止世界大会で、初めて自分の被爆体験を語った。これが谷口さんの転機となる。それからは国内だけでなく世界各地で、核兵器廃絶の願いを人びとに訴え続けている。二度と自分のような被爆者をつくりだしてはならないと――。

　この年、29歳。結婚というもう一つの転機があった。夫人は父親の仕事の関係で朝鮮にいたため、被爆を免れた。当初、谷口さんの傷跡のあまりの酷さに衝撃を受けたが、夫がこうむった体と心の傷を癒すために、温かい家庭をつくることで懸命に支えた。一男一女にも恵まれ、つらい日々にも幸せが訪れる。

　谷口さんの背中の皮膚は、今でも組織が壊れたままで発汗できず、少しでも体重が増えると、癒着したケロイドが張り裂けるように痛む。

　1974年から、谷口さんらは「核実験に抗議する長崎市民の会」を結成し、核実験に対する抗議の座り込みを行なってきた。世界のあちこちで核実験が行なわれる度に、松山町の平和記念像前に集まり、抗議の座り込みを行なう。谷口さんは「市民の会」の代表として行動の先頭に立つ。この30年間、雨の日も風の日も休むことなく、400回近い抗議を重ねてきた。被爆者だけでなく、一般の老人も、若者も、子どもたちも、観光に訪れた人たちも、心を一つにして座り込む。

　その中には、夫人や娘さん、そして可愛い孫たちの姿もある。

その日まで

　2004年8月9日――「長崎原爆の日」に、ロシアはこの年、複数回の臨界前核実験を実施したことを明らかにした。アメリカは強大な核兵器保持のための臨界前核実験を続けるだけでなく、使える「小型核兵器」の開発を進めている。新たな核兵器開発競争は一向に歯止めがかからない。

　「長崎原爆被災者協議会」の副会長の重責も担う谷口さんは語る。

　「被爆60年を迎えようとする今、被爆者の高齢化が進みます。あの日、熱線・爆風・放射能を浴びた被爆者は、急激にその数を減らしました。被爆者を援護する取り組みも、急がねばなりません。そして核兵器のない平和な世界を実現するために、今は〈願いから行動へ〉の時です。それに若い世代に運動をバトンタッチしていく時でもあります。私たち被爆者は生きている限り、そのために命を燃やし続けます」

　体調を維持するために夏の強い日差しを避けながら、毎日、活動を続ける谷口さんの表情に、核廃絶へ向けての強い決意が込められていた。

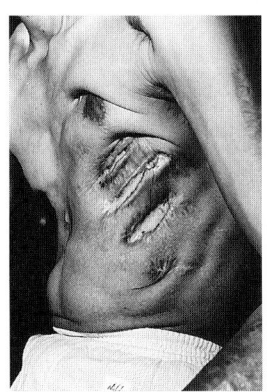

回復しない谷口さんの胸部。背中の全面大火傷でうつぶせのままで寝かされていたため、床擦れで筋肉が削げ落ちてしまった。

The wounds on Mr. Taniguchi's chest that will never heal. Bedsores and muscle atrophy were caused by the extended convalescence for the severe burns on his back.

Taniguchi Sumiteru, "As Long as There is Life"

Text and photos by Kurosaki Haruo, Nagasaki branch of the Japan Realist Photographers Association

Overcoming Excruciating Pain

Mr. Taniguchi (1929 ~), a resident of Nagasaki, was on his bicycle delivering the mail in Sumiyoshi-cho, 1.8 kilometers from ground zero, when the bomb was dropped. He was a sixteen year old mailman at the time.

The skin was burned off his back, leaving it an open wound, and from his left shoulder down to his hand the skin dangled loosely. He took shelter in the nearby underground facilities of the Mitsubishi munitions plant, where he had the annoying draping folds of skin clipped off. He was reached three days later by a rescue team, and then moved from one first-aid station to the next before finally being admitted to the naval hospital in the city of Omura.

He spent the next year and nine months lying face down, unable to move due to the severe burns on his back from the heat rays released by the atomic bomb. The muscles of his chest, left cheek, and chin atrophied during this extended period of convalescence.

Upon his release from the hospital in 1949, he returned to work, but the pain from his injuries forced him to take sick leave repeatedly for continued hospital treatment. To this day the skin on Mr. Taniguchi's back does not function properly and is unable to excrete sweat. Furthermore, any weight gain causes a painful tearing sensation in the keloids that scar his back.

In spite of his injuries, Mr. Taniguchi has crusaded tirelessly for the abolition of nuclear weapons. In 1956, at the age of 29, he participated in the founding of the Nagasaki Atomic Bomb Youth Association and, at the World Conference Against Atomic and Hydrogen Bombs, he spoke publicly for the first time of his experience of the bombing. This event marked a turned point in his life. Since that day, both in Japan and throughout the world, he has continued to voice his hopes for the abolition of nuclear weapons. He asks simply that the world never again expose others to the atomic bomb.

The year 1956 also brought another important event: marriage. The woman who was to be his wife had accompanied her father to Korea on business and had therefore escaped the bombing. Shocked though she was at the horrific scars Mr. Taniguchi still carried, she set out determinedly to create a loving home to ease her hasband's physical and psychological pain. The couple was blessed with both a son and a daughter, who brought joy into their trying days.

In 1974 Mr. Taniguchi joined others in forming an organization called Nagasaki Citizen's Opposed to Nuclear Testing . Whenever a nuclear test is carried out somewhere in the world, this group gathers in front of the Peace Memorial in Matsuyama-chô to hold a sit-down demonstration as an expression of their opposition. Mr. Taniguchi, as the representative of this citizen's group, takes a leading role. Over the past thirty years, through rain and shine, he has never missed a single one of the almost 400 such demonstrations in which atomic bomb victims are joined by the elderly, the young, children, and even tourists visiting the area. All are united in a single cause. Among the crowds at these demonstrations one can often spot his wife, his daughter, and even his precious grandchildren.

2004年8月9日、無縁仏の碑に詣でる谷口さん。長崎の被爆で、およそ7万人の人びとが犠牲となった。人知れず亡くなった人びとを慰霊する無縁仏の碑があちこちに建立されている。

Mr. Taniguchi paying his respects at a memorial to unidentified fatalities. Approximately 70,000 people died in the atomic bombing of Nagasaki. Dotting the city landscape are memorials erected in memory of those whose remains were never identified. 9 August 2004.

'Til That Day Comes

On 9 August 2004, the anniversary of the atomic bombing of Nagasaki, Russia announced that it had that year performed multiple nuclear weapons tests. The United States, for its part, not only continues the nuclear testing necessary to maintain its enormous arsenal of nuclear weapons, but is also moving forward with the development of smaller deployable nuclear weapons. The nuclear arms race continues unabated.

Mr. Taniguchi, speaking as the deputy chair of the Nagasaki Council of A-Bomb Sufferers, commented: "Today, sixty years after the atomic bombings, we are faced with an aging population of atomic bomb victims. The number of individuals exposed to the blast, the heat rays, and the radiation that day and still living now is dropping rapidly. We must work quickly in our campaign to support those victims. If we are to realize our dreams for a peaceful world devoid of nuclear weapons, we must act on those dreams. The time is now. It is also important at this juncture to pass the baton on to the younger generation. As long as there is life in us, we victims of the atomic bombs will continue to work passionately towards these ends."

Though Mr. Taniguchi now avoids the hot rays of the summer sun in order to maintain the delicate balance of his health, he continues to work daily for the abolition of nuclear weapons. His deep commitment to this cause is etched into the very lines of his face.

外国人
被爆者

韓国人被爆者・林玉仙さん　大邱市
在住。1936年5月12日生まれ。広島
市観音町で被爆。「原爆に遭った時、
家族は7人で、私は10歳でした。被爆
してから手足がしだいに萎縮して、
こんな姿になりました」（撮影／1984
〜1987年頃・伊藤孝司）

Im Ok Sun, Korean Atomic Bomb
Victim.
Born on 12 May 1936, Ms. Im now
resides in the city of Daegu in Korea.
She was in Kannon-machi, Hiroshima,
when the bomb was dropped. "I was
ten years old and part of a family of
seven when I experienced the atomic
bomb. My hands and feet began to
shrivel up at that time, and I am left
with them disfigured as you see
today." (Photo by Ito Takashi ,
sometime between 1984 and 1987.)

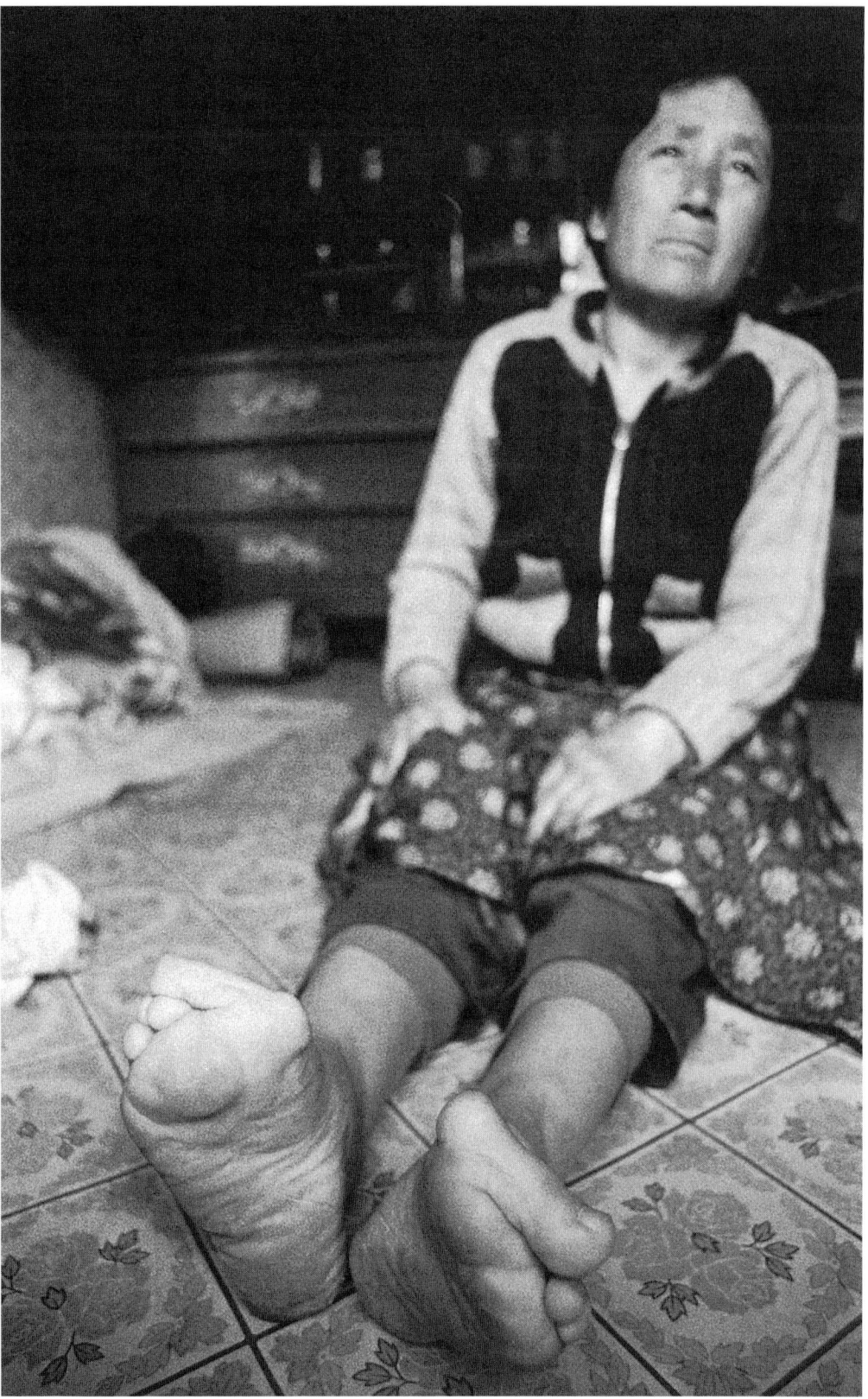

Non-Japanese Victims of the Atomic Bombs

丸木位里・俊の「原爆の図」第13部「米軍捕虜の死」でも明らかなように、「ヒロシマ」「ナガサキ」で犠牲になったのは日本人だけではなかった。20数名のアメリカ人捕虜をはじめ、現在分かっているだけでも、朝鮮人（韓国人）、中国人、イギリス人、オーストラリア人、オランダ人、インドネシア人、マレーシア人が原爆の被害を受けている。

その実数は、正確な記録＝資料が消失したこともあって定かではないが、数万人といわれている朝鮮人（韓国人）をはじめ数人、数十人、数百人規模で、外国人が「ヒロシマ」「ナガサキ」の犠牲となった。彼らは、日本が36年間植民地にしていた朝鮮半島から「強制連行」で連れてこられたり、職を求めてやってきた人びとであり、アジア・太平洋戦争で日本が占領したマレーシアやフィリピン、インドネシアなどのアジア各地から派遣された「南方特別留学生」やアジア・太平洋の戦場で捕虜となり、労働力不足の日本に連れてこられた兵士たちであった。

彼らのうち何人が死に、何人がその後祖国に帰って充分な治療も受けられず、「被爆者」として苦しみ続けたのか。日本人被爆者には不充分ではあるが、一定の「保障」がなされ、また「被爆者援護法」によって原爆病の治療も行なわれていることと比較して、いかに彼ら外国人被爆者が戦後厳しい状況に置かれてきたことか。それもこれも原爆を投下したアメリカ軍を中心とする占領軍の下で、原爆＝被爆に関する情報が秘密扱いになっていた状況下で、外国人被爆者の実態も充分に明らかにされてこなかったからに他ならない。戦後の東西冷戦構造を象徴する核軍拡競争下にあって、核＝原爆が人種や民族、さらには国境も越えて人間や地球環境を脅かす悲惨な状況をもたらすものであるという事実は、できるだけ伏せられていたのである。

その意味で「ヒロシマ・ナガサキ」における外国人被爆者は、その後世界の各地、例えばロンゲラップ島やムルロワ環礁など南太平洋におけるアメリカ、ソ連、フランス、イギリスの核実験場となった近辺の島々に出現した「ヒバクシャ」や自国の核実験場や核施設が生み出した「ヒバクシャ」の先駆をなすものであった。

As we can see in artists Maruki Iri and Toshi's "Death of American Prisoners-of War (painting 13 in their "Hiroshima Panels")", it was not only Japanese nationals who suffered in the atomic bombings of Hiroshima and Nagasaki. At this point in time we know that in addition to over twenty American POWs, individuals from Korea, China, England, Australia, Holland, Indonesia, and Malaysia were also rendered victims of the atomic bombs.

Precise records and pertinent materials have disappeared, leaving exact numbers impossible to calculate. Nevertheless, it is believed that Korean victims number in the tens of thousands, and the figures for other foreign nationals range from single digits to the hundreds. Some of these victims were brought to Japan as forced labor from the Korean penninsula, which was under Japanese colonial rule for thirty-six years; others came of their own accord seeking employment; still others were "special exchange students from the southern islands," people dispatched to Japan from Malaysia, the Phillipines, Indonesia and other parts of Asia occupied by Japan during the Pacific War. There were also soldiers captured on the battlefields of Asia and the Pacific and forcibly brought to Japan to ease the labor shortage on the main islands.

How many of these people died? How many returned to their homelands to face a lifetime of suffering as an atomic bomb victim without access to proper health care? However insufficient it may be, Japanese victims of the atomic bombs have at least received some compensation and have benefitted from legislation that provides for treatment of atomic bomb-related illnesses. What type of trying conditions, though, have the non-Japanese victims faced? All of these issues remain unresolved. The actual conditions faced by the non-Japanese victims remain clouded in mystery because the Occupation Forces, led by the very Americans who dropped the bombs, have treated as "secret" all information related to the bombs and their victims. Caught in the nuclear arms race at the core of Cold War politics, the truth about the threat posed by those weapons has been largely hidden. Too many would have us remain ignorant of the manner in which those weapons (and nuclear power in general) transcend all boundaries of race, ethnicity and nation in the misery they bring and the grave danger they pose to humankind and the global environment.

These non-Japanese victims of the atomic bombs at Hiroshima and Nagasaki are tragically but the first of many. There are already other victims around the world: those exposed to radiation while on the Rongelap and Mururoa Atolls during the nuclear tests conducted in the South Pacific by the United States, France, the Soviet Union, and England as well as those victimized by the nuclear experiments and power plants right here in Japan.

広島を何度も歩いた

広河隆一

惨劇の記憶の中心部は美しい平和公園によって覆われ、目で見える痕跡は原爆ドームだけだ。大地の下に焼け爛れた町がそのまま埋まっていることなど、想像力を超えていて、なかなか実感がわかない。しかし路地を歩くと、いたるところにゆかりの地蔵が立ち、町に住む人々にとっては、記憶の記念碑は散在して生活を取り囲んでいる。

美しい公園は、死者の鎮魂のために、必要なのかもしれない。もし広島で核の問題が終わっているなら、それもいいのかもしれない。しかし、日々想像力が枯渇していく毎日を送っている私たちには、核の恐ろしさをもっと生々しく記憶する必要があるように思える。

日本人から広島の記憶が遠ざかる一方で、今でも世界の多くの人々は、広島・長崎を核の犠牲の地としっかり認識している。彼らは日本人が被害者の側から核を考えることができる稀有な国民だと信じている。ところが残念なことに広島の名は、ときに原発産業の正当化のために利用されたりする。チェルノブイリ原発事故の被害調査でも、広島の医学者が原発事故の汚染の危険性を軽んじて報告し、結果的に病気の早期発見の道が遠のき、多くの被害者が出たということもある。核爆弾が広島と長崎に投下されてから60年。そして2006年にはチェルノブイリ事故から20年になる。核の問題はたった一歩の解決も見ていない。被害がこれほど長く続くことも誰が予想できただろうか。

広島を歩くたびに私は、かつてある詩人が歌ったように、大地の下にはおびただしい死者が眠っているから、足音を忍ばせて、歩かなければならない、と自分に言い聞かせている。

ひろかわ・りゅういち　1943年、中国・天津生まれ。フォトジャーナリスト。イスラエル、中東諸国を中心に海外取材を重ね、レバノン戦争とパレスチナ人キャンプの虐殺事件の記録で、よみうり写真大賞（1982）、チェルノブイリ・スリーマイル島原発事故の報告で、講談社出版文化賞（1989）、『人間の戦場』（新潮社）で日本ジャーナリスト会議特別賞を受賞（1998）。『チェルノブイリ　消えた458の村』（日本図書センター）、『パレスチナ』（岩波書店）など著書多数。また2004年3月より報道写真誌「DAYS　JAPAN」を発刊、編集長を務める。

Walking Hiroshima, Again and Again

Hirokawa Ryuichi

My memories of that tragedy center on the area now covered by the beautiful Peace Park, and the only visible remnant of that day is the Atomic Bomb Dome. Though the burnt rubble of the city as it was that day is now buried beneath this peaceful landscape, the fact is impossible for me to imagine. It seems somehow unreal. At every turn in the road, however, stand statutes of *Jizo*, the boddhisattva helping all living things to salvation, and the residents of the city live their lives surrounded by these and other scattered memorials to that memory.

The gorgeous park may indeed be necessary to console the souls of the dead. I would appreciate it as such if but the nuclear issues that Hiroshima represents had been resolved. The fact of the matter, however, is that with each passing day our ability to conceive of what transpired there fades even more. I believe what we need is something that more vividly reminds us of the horror of nuclear reactions.

While the memory of what happened at Hiroshima dims in the minds of the Japanese, people around the world even today are keenly aware that Hiroshima and Nagasaki were victims of nuclear weapons. These people hold the belief that the Japanese are unique in their ability to ponder nuclear issues from the perspective of the victim. The truth, however, is that Hiroshima is often invoked in the defense of the nuclear energy industry. For example, called upon during the investigation of the nuclear meltdown at Chernobyl, medical professionals from Hiroshima understated the potential environmental threat caused by the accident. This resulted in a failure to make early diagnoses, thereby increasing the suffering of victims. It has been sixty years since the bombs were dropped on Hiroshima and Nagasaki. The year 2006 will mark the twenty year anniversary of the accident at Chernobyl. In this time absolutely no progress has been made in addressing the threat posed by nuclear reactions. Who among us could have imagined that we would remain victims of things nuclear for so long?

Every time I walk the streets of Hiroshima I murmur the words of the poet who once wrote: "Walk softly, for beneath this great earth rest the souls of the uncountable dead."

Hirokawa Ryuichi. Born in Tianjin, China, in 1943, is an international photojournalist who has worked mainly in Israel and the Middle East. His coverage of violence in Lebanon and the atrocities in Palestinian refugee camps garnered him the Yomiuri Grand Prix for photography, his reporting of the accidents at the nuclear power plants in Chernobyl and Three Mile Island earned him the Kodansha Cultural Prize, and his book *Ningen no senjo* (The human battlefield, Shinchosha, 1988) won him a special award from the Japanese Congress of Journalists. Hirokawa's other publications include *Cherunobuiri: kieta 458 no mura* (Chernobyl: The 458 villages that vanished, Nihon Tosho Center, 1999) and *Paresuchina* (Palestine, Iwanami shoten, 2002). Beginning in March 2004 he will serve as publisher and editor-in-chief of *Days Japan*, a magazine dedicated to photojournalism.

核なき世界を求めて

The Quest for a World Free of Nuclear Hazards

相生橋の復旧工事 1946年、欄干が吹き飛ばされ、路面が著しく傷ついた相生橋を復旧する、とりあえずの応急工事が始まった。75年間は人も住めないと言われた広島の復興に市民は夢を抱いた。被爆者は原爆による傷病に苦しみ、疎開からの帰郷者、復員兵、引揚者など被爆をまぬがれた人たちも、飢餓とインフレに追い詰められていた。（撮影／岸本吉太）

Reconstruction of Aioi Bridge.
In 1946 people set to work on the Aioi Bridge, repairing the railings that had been blown off in the blast and smoothing the damaged surface of the roadway. Undaunted by the prediction that it would be 75 years before people could live again in Hiroshima, these residents of the city acted on their dream of its rebirth. In addition to the atomic bomb victims suffering from injuries and illnesses, the population included former residents who had evacuated to outlying areas, repatriated soldiers, and returning colonials, all of whom had escaped the bomb. Without exception, though, residents of the city battled food shortages and inflation. (Photo by Kishimoto Kichita .)

闇市 天皇の神格否定宣言、新憲法発布、連合軍による戦争犯罪の追及…1946年、戦後2年目の日本は激変のなかにあった。食糧難にあえぐ広島でも、他の都市と同じく闇市に人が群がった。（撮影／1946年春・山端庸介）

Black Market. Things changed rapidly in Japan in 1946, the first year after the war: the Emperor renounced his divinity, the new Constitution was promulgated, and the Allied Forces prosecuted the war criminals. Hiroshima, like other cities, faced severe food shortages, and throngs of people rushed to the black markets. (Photo by Yamahata Yosuke, Spring 1946.)

雪をほおばる子どもたち　1950年、
「放射能があるから食べちゃいけんよ」
と大人たちは心配するが、子どもたち
は無心に爆心地の雪をほおばった。
（撮影／佐々木雄一郎）

Children Gobbling Snow.
Though adults in 1950 warned them
about the radiation absorbed by the
snow, children gobbled it down even
in the area of ground zero. (Photo by
Sasaki Yuichiro.)

第五福竜丸乗組員・久保山愛吉さんの死　1954年9月23日、久保山さんは東京第一病院で放射能障害によって死亡した。東京駅から故郷・焼津に向かう遺骨を前に、夫人と3人の娘、遺影の後ろに母の姿も。（提供／毎日新聞社）

Death of Kuboyama Aikichi, Crew of the Fishing Vessel "Lucky Dragon" (Fukuryumaru).
On 23 September 1954 Mr. Kuboyama died of radiation poisoning at the First National Hospital of Tokyo. This photo shows Kuboyama's wife and three children as they accompany his remains from Tokyo to his hometown of Yaizu, Shizuoka. Behind Kuboyama's photograph, held by his daughter, stands the mother of the deceased. (Photo courtesy of the Mainichi Newspapers.)

全国に広がる署名運動　1954年4月、東京・上野公園で。（提供／機関紙連合通信社）

Signature Collection Campaigns Around the Country.
Ueno Park, Tokyo. April 1954. (Photo courtesy of the Rengo News Agency.)

　1954年3月1日のアメリカによるビキニ島での水爆実験で被曝した第五福竜丸の事件をきっかけに、東京杉並の主婦たちを中心に始まった「原水爆禁止運動」は、被爆地「広島・長崎」における平和運動や国内の反戦運動と連動して、翌年の8月には第1回の原水爆禁止世界大会を開くまでに成長していった。「ヒロシマ・ナガサキ」を原点とし、「反核」「平和」を願う人びとが支え続け、現在も続いているこの運動は、アメリカとソ連だけでなく、イギリスがいち早く核保有国の仲間入りをし（1952年2月）、その後フランスが（1960年2月）、そして中国が（1964年10月）核保有国となるような世界情勢に異議申し立てを行なうものであった。

　しかし、「東側」を形成するソ連と中国の反目（中ソ論争）をきっかけに、それぞれの国を支持する日本共産党系と社会党・総評系に分裂し、反核の力をそぐことになる。だが、それとは別にアメリカがヨーロッパに配備しようとしたパーシングⅡ巡航ミサイルによってもたらされた、1980年代初めの「核戦争の危機」に対する世界各国の反核運動（日本では「文学者の反核運動」に象徴される）は、多くの人びとが核＝原爆の恐ろしさ・非人間性を認識していることの証でもあった。「核廃絶」は、この地球と人類の未来を憂う人びとの、緊急かつ切実な願いにほかならない。

第1回原水爆禁止世界大会　1955年8月6日、海外14か国から52人が、日本全国から2,575人が参加。「…原水爆が禁止され、人類の上に真の平和がくる日まで運動を展開していく」と宣言した。（提供／中国新聞社刊『被爆50年写真集　ヒロシマの記録』）

The First World Conference Against Atomic and Hydrogen Bombs. The conference, held on 6 August 1955, was attended by 2,575 Japanese nationals and 52 foreign guests from 14 different nations. The conference declared its members' intention to "continue this campaign until the day that atomic and hydrogen bombs are abolished and a true peace settles upon the earth." (Provided courtesy of the Chugoku Shimbun Newspaper.)

ニューヨークの反核100万人デモ　1982年6月12日。「東西冷戦」が「熱い戦争」に転化するかという危機感が世界をおおった。NATO（北大西洋条約機構）が決定した対ソ戦略に対して反核運動が世界を席巻。日本からも1,200名がデモに参加した。（撮影／尾辻弥寿雄）

New York's Million People March Against Nuclear Weapons. The world-wide fear that the Cold War might turn "hot" came to a peak when NATO announced a new strategy for dealing with the Soviet Union. Anti-nuclear movements responded vigorously. Japanese participants in this 12 June 1982 demonstration in New York numbered around 1,200. (Photo by Otsuji Yasuo.)

On 1 March 1954 the United States tested a hydrogen bomb near the Bikini Atoll, exposing the crew of the Japanese fishing vessel "Lucky Dragon" (Fukuryumaru) to the fallout. In response, housewives in Suginami, Tokyo, started a movement opposed to atomic and hydrogen bombs. This organization later joined forces with peace movements in Hiroshima and Nagasaki, the cities destroyed by the atomic bomb, as well as anti-war movements across the nation. The coordination of these groups made possible the first World Conference Against Atomic and Hydrogen Bombs, which convened in August of the following year. Rooted in the tragedies of Hiroshima and Nagasaki but supported by all peace-loving people opposed to nuclear weapons, this organization continues to voice its objections to nuclear proliferation around the world. Though the United States and Soviet Union were the first nations to develop nuclear arsenals, others were not far behind. They were soon joined by Great Britain

(February 1952), France (February 1960) and China (October 1964).

Regrettably the hostility between the two major countries in the eastern bloc, the Soviet Union and China, prompted a similar split between their respective supporters in Japan, the Japan Communist Party and the Socialist Party/Labor Union. This discord slowed the anti-nuclear movement. On the other hand, the attempt by the United States to position Pershing II cruise missiles in Europe raised international awareness of the danger of nuclear war, and the anti-nuclear groups that sprouted across the globe in the early 1980s are proof that an increasing number of people are realizing the threat posed to humanity. For people concerned about the future of humankind and the earth, the abolition of nuclear weapons and power plants is the most urgent and pressing item on their agenda.

崩壊したチェルノブイリ原子力発電所
1986年4月26日午前1時23分、巨大な爆発音がウクライナの闇に轟いた。崩壊した炉心から大量の放射能が噴出し、処理作業員に限っても、その後の14年間に5万5,000人が死亡した。住民13万人は汚染地域からの移住を余儀なくされ、今も甲状腺障害、異常出産、先天性ガンなどの障害に苦しむ。すでに400基を超える原子力発電所が地球上に建設され、日本も52基に達している。(提供／毎日新聞社)

Ruins of the Nuclear Reactor at Chernobyl. At 1:23 a.m. on the night of 26 April 1986 the sound of a huge explosion resounded through the Ukranian night. The meltdown of the reactor's core released massive amounts of radiation into the environment and, over the next 14 years, 55,000 workers from the plant died. Contamination of the area forced 130,000 people to evacuate, and this population continues to be plagued by thyroid disorders, congenital cancers, and birth defects. There are now over 400 such nuclear reactors across the globe, 52 of which are located in Japan. (Photo courtesy of the Mainichi Newspapers.)

ベルリンの壁崩壊　1989年11月9日。ソ連のペレストロイカ政策を契機に民主化の激流が東欧、ソ連をも押し流した。第2次世界大戦後、核兵器拡大の背景だった冷戦構造は崩れ、ヒロシマ・ナガサキを原点とする「核時代」は新たな局面を迎えたはずだった。(提供／毎日新聞社)

The Fall of the Berlin Wall. 9 November 1989. The Soviet policy of perestroika inspired democratic movements domestically as well as throughout eastern Europe. One result was the fall of the Berlin Wall on 9 November 1989. The collapse of the post-WW II Cold War system that had driven nuclear proliferation marked the beginning of a new stage in the "nuclear age" that had begun with the bombings of Hiroshima and Nagasaki. (Photo courtesy of the Mainichi Newspapers.)

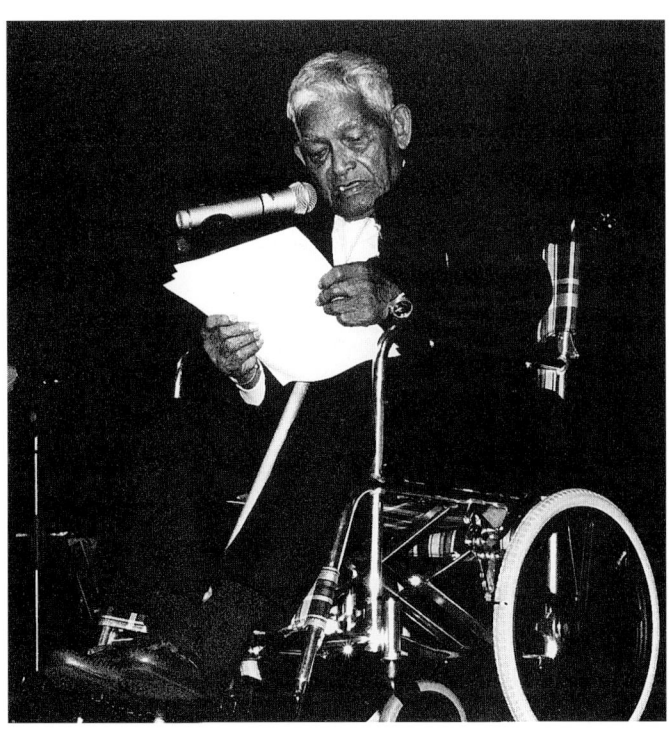

ビキニ被曝村長・アンジャインさんの死　1954年3月1日、マーシャル諸島・ビキニ環礁で行なわれたアメリカの水爆実験で、日本のマグロ漁船「第五福竜丸」の乗組員たちが被曝したが、アンジャインさんも村長をしていたロンゲラップ島で「死の灰」を浴びていた。被曝後、80人の村民と共に米軍に収容され、マジュロ環礁に移住させられた。3年後、アメリカ政府の安全宣言で帰島したが、住民に異常出産が多発。彼自身も吐血が続いた。1972年に19歳で死亡した実の息子は「水爆死第1号」とアメリカも認めていた。長年、アメリカ政府に被曝の補償や汚染除去を要求。たびたび来日して「反核・反戦」の運動を日本人と共にした。2004年7月20日、ハワイの療養先で81歳の生涯を閉じた。写真は2004年3月、焼津で行われた第五福竜丸被曝記念集会に参加し、核の廃絶を訴えるアンジャインさん。死の4か月前のことだった。(撮影／豊崎博光)

The Death of Mayor Anjain, Exposed to Nuclear Radiation on the Bikini Atoll. The crew members of the Japanese tuna trawler "Lucky Dragon" (Fukuryumaru) were not the only victims of the United States' hydrogen bomb test on the Bikini Atoll in the Marshall Islands on 1 March 1954. This test also rained nuclear fallout on the island of Rongelap. After the hydrogen bomb test Mayor Anjain and eighty other island residents were first detained by U.S. troops, and later forcibly relocated to the Majuro Atoll. When the U.S. declared Rongelap safe three years later, they returned to the island, only to see a sharp increase in birth defects. When Mr Anjain's son died in 1972 at the age of nineteen, even the Americans recognized him as the first victim of the hydrogen bomb. Mr. Anjain waged a long battle with the U.S. government for reparations and environmental clean-up; he also visited Japan frequently to participate in various anti-nuclear rallies and demonstrations for peace. He himself suffered bouts of illness wherein he would vomit blood. Mayor Anjain died on 20 July 2004, at the age of 81, while convalescing in Hawaii.
This photo, taken at a gathering held in Yaizu, Shizuoka, to commemorate the Lucky Dragon tragedy, shows Mr. Anjain pleading for the abolition of all things nuclear. It was taken four months before his death. (Photo by Toyosaki Hiromitsu.)

世界の核兵器 Nuclear Weapons Around the World

『ストックホルム国際平和研究所年鑑・2003年版』などより
Stockholm International Peace Research Institute Yearbook (2003)

●核兵器保有国 Nations Possessing Nuclear Weapons

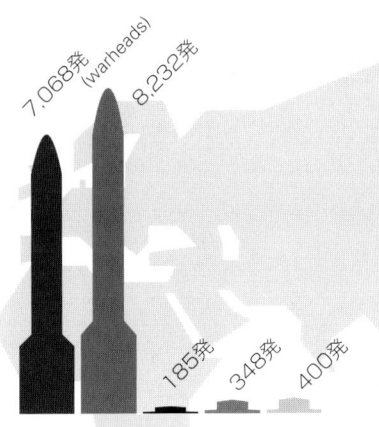

7,068発 (warheads)
8,232発
185発
348発
400発

アメリカ USA
ロシア Russia
イギリス UK
フランス France
中国 China

●実質的核兵器保有国 Officially Unrecognized Nuclear Powers

インド India	30〜150発 (warheads)	
パキスタン Pakistan	30〜50発	
イスラエル Israel	200〜300発	

●核保有疑惑国 Nations Suspected of Having Nuclear Capabilities

北朝鮮 North Korea

「6か国協議」のなかで核兵器開発計画の放棄を迫られているが、「核抑止力を保持している」と発言、2010年までに200発以上を製造する能力を持っていると見られている。＊2005年2月10日、北朝鮮は核兵器製造の宣言を行なった。

イラン Iran

2004年、国際原子力機関の査察をいったん受け入れるが、ウラン濃縮に使用する遠心分離機の組み立てを再開すると通告。

●核兵器計画・核兵器を放棄した国 Nations That Have Relinquished Nuclear Weapons or Plans to Obtain Them.

イラク　南アフリカ共和国　リビア　ブラジル　アルゼンチン

ウクライナ　ベラルーシ　カザフスタン（ソ連崩壊後、ロシアに移管）

ルーマニア　アルジェリア　スウェーデン

Iraq, South Africa, Libya, Brazil, Argentina
Ukraine, Belarus, Kazakhstan (under Russian jurisdiction since the collapse of the USSR)
Romania, Algeria, Sweden

この地球上には、今なお3万発近くの核兵器が存在し、その95%以上をアメリカ、ロシアの両国が保有、およそ半数の1万5000発がいつでも使用できる状態で配備されていると推定されている（アメリカNRDC＝天然資源防衛評議会の「ニュークリア・ノートブック」より。ほぼ上図の数字と照応する）。

2001年9月11日、ニューヨークを襲った同時多発テロを契機に、アメリカは軍事戦略を2つの点で変化させた。

1つは、アメリカが攻撃される可能性があると判断した国に対しては、攻撃される前に攻撃する「先制攻撃戦略」を打ち出したこと。2003年に始まるイラク戦争は、その具体化の第一歩だった。もう1つは、新たな小型兵器開発を急いでいることである。「小型化」すれば、住民への被害を小さくでき「使いやすい」というのが開発の理由だが、現有する原爆が平均して広島型の10倍以上の爆発力であることを前提とした「小型化」に過ぎない。

この2つの戦略が結びついた「先制核攻撃」の危険を、2004年8月に発せられたヒロシマおよびナガサキの「平和宣言」は強く訴えている。

Nuclear Weapons in the World Today

The National Resource Defense Council's "Nuclear Notebook" estimates that the world today is home to almost 30,000 nuclear warheads, 95% of which are in either the United States or Russia, and roughly half (15,000) are deployable at any time.

Since the multiple terrorist attacks targeting New York on 11 September 2001, the United States has made two adjustments to their military strategy. The first is to employ pre-emptive strikes, i.e. attacks against nations they determine might potentially threaten the United States. The war in Iraq, which began in 2003, is the first concrete example of that new strategy. The second strategic adjustment is the decision to hasten the development of new, smaller nuclear weapons. The justification for this development is that smaller nuclear weapons are more easily deployed and would decrease casualties among non-combatants. It is important to realize that in this case the word "smaller" is used relative to the nuclear weapons currently stockpiled, any of which has on average a destructive force ten times that of the bomb dropped on Hiroshima.

The call for peace issued by Hiroshima and Nagasaki in August 2004 is directed against the new threat posed by the logical union of those two new strategies: a pre-emptive nuclear strike.

もう一つの福竜丸のこと

松谷みよ子

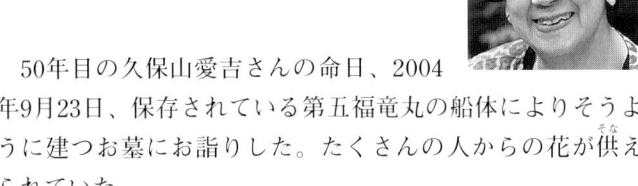

50年目の久保山愛吉さんの命日、2004年9月23日、保存されている第五福竜丸の船体によりそうように建つお墓にお詣りした。たくさんの人からの花が供えられていた。

1954年、アメリカはマーシャル諸島で水爆実験を重ね、日本のマグロ漁船第五福竜丸が被曝、無線長の久保山愛吉さんが亡くなったことは、多くの人びとの記憶にある。

しかし、私は第五福竜丸だけではない、数知れぬマグロ漁船が被曝していたこと、そしてそのうちの一人の青年、藤井節弥さんのことを知らなかった。2002年、千葉のお寺で行なわれた〈広島・長崎の火を守る集い〉に参加の帰途、友人の山口義夫さんがとつとつと節弥さんの生涯を語ってくれた。電車に並んで座りながら聞いたこの話が忘れ難く、今年もう一度山口さんに語ってもらい、テープに収めた。

"節弥はね、1945年8月9日、長崎に落とされた原爆に、小学生のとき被曝したんだ。母親と姉と高知の実家に帰ったけど、納屋(なや)の暮らしで、高校卒業した年「お母さん、僕が働いてお母さんに家を建ててあげる」って、マグロ漁船に乗り込んで、ビキニの実験にぶっかって、また被曝したわけ。怖くなってマグロ漁船を降りたけど、身体はやられてるし仕事も見つからない。家を建てるって約束したから、また三浦岬でマグロ漁船に乗船し、また核実験に逢う。怖い怖いと海に飛びこみ、久里浜の病院に入れられるんだけど、久里浜の海に入水自殺するんだよね"

アメリカは1962年まで100回実験を繰り返したという。全国にどれほどの節弥さんがいるのだろう。

まつたに・みよこ　1926年、東京生まれ。童話作家。坪田譲治に師事、民話を再創造した『龍の子太郎』(1960)で国際アンデルセン賞優良賞を受賞。『ちいさいモモちゃん』(講談社)、広島の被爆者を描いた『ふたりのイーダ』(講談社)、『私のアンネ=フランク』(偕成社)など作品多数。また『現代民話考』(全12巻、ちくま文庫)、『現代の民話』(中公新書)など、現代社会で生まれ語り、継がれる新たな民話に光を当てる。

Another "Lucky Dragon" (Fukuryumaru)

Matsutani Miyoko

On 23 September 2004, the fiftieth anniversary of Kuboyama Aikichi's death, I went to pay my respects at his grave, located beside his ship, the "Lucky Dragon #5" (Fukuryûmaru #5), which has been preserved. The grave was covered with flowers brought there as offerings by so many people.

Most of us remember how the numerous hydrogen bomb tests conducted by the United States on the Marshall Islands in 1954 exposed the Japanese tuna trawler to radiation and caused the death of its captain, Kuboyama Aikichi. What is little known, however, is that the "Lucky Dragon" was but one of countless fishing vessels exposed to the radiation emitted by these tests. On one of them was a young man named Fujii Setsuya. I first heard about Setsuya in 2002, on my way home from the Gathering to Protect the Flame of Hiroshima and Nagasaki. A friend of his named Yamaguchi Yoshio told me something of Setsuya's life as I sat beside him on the train. What I heard was a moving tale, and I had Mr. Yamaguchi repeat it last year so that I might record it.

"Setsuya was a student in Nagasaki when the atomic bomb was dropped on 9 August 1945," said Mr. Yamaguchi. "Along with his elder sister and mother, Setsuya evacuated the city and returned to their ancestral home in Kôchi, on the island of Shikoku, where they lived in a barn. The year he graduated from high school Setsuya told his mother that he would get a job and someday build her a proper home. He promptly took work on a tuna trawler, and that is how he happened to be in the Bikini Atoll at the time of the hydrogen bomb test. This incident was his second exposure to radiation from an atomic bomb. Unnerved, he left the trawler, but he was now in poor health and unable to find other employment. Having promised his mother a proper home, he went back to his old line of work, this time on a fishing vessel sailing out of the Miura Cape. It was while serving on this ship that he was again caught up in an atomic bomb test, and he was so afraid that he jumped into the sea. He was later admitted to the hospital at Kurihama, only to later drown himself in the waters nearby."

By the year 1962 the United States had already conducted a hundred nuclear weapons tests. How Setsuyas might there be out there?

Matsutani Miyoko, a writer of children's books, was born in Tokyo in 1926. After studying with writer Tsubota Joji, she was awarded a place on the International Hans Christian Andersen Honor List with her re-telling of a folktale in *Taro: The Dragon Boy* (Kodansha International, 1967; Tatsu no Ko Taro, 1960). Her many other works include *Chiisai Momo-chan* (Little Momo-chan, Kodansha, 1964), *Watashi no Anne Furanku* (My Anne Frank, Kaiseisha, 1979), and *Two Little Girls Called Iida* (Kodansha, 1985; Futari no Iida, 1969), which depicts victims of the atomic bomb. Matsutani has also called attention to the modern folktales told in contemporary society with her *Gendai minwako* (Thoughts on contemporary folktales, 12 volumes, Chikuma bunko) and *Gendai no minwa* (Contemporary folktales, Chuko shinsho, 2000).

原爆・核に関する略年譜

1941年	10月	アメリカ大統領ルーズベルト、原子爆弾の研究・開発を決定。
1942年	6月	アメリカ、原爆の開発を「マンハッタン計画」として推進。
1945年	7月	16日 アメリカ、ニューメキシコ州で世界初の原爆実験に成功。
		アメリカ大統領トルーマン、原爆投下を命令、投下候補地として広島、小倉、新潟、長崎。
	8月	6日午前8時15分 広島に原爆（ウラニウム型）を投下。
		9日午前11時2分 長崎に原爆（プルトニウム型）を投下。
1946年	7月	アメリカ、ビキニ環礁で原爆水中爆発実験。
1949年	8月	ソ連、初の原爆実験。
1950年	1月	トルーマン大統領、水爆製造を命令。
	6月	朝鮮戦争始まる。11月 トルーマン、原爆使用検討を言明。
1951年	9月	対日講和条約・日米安保条約調印。
1952年	2月	イギリス、原爆保有を公表（10月 南太平洋モンテベロ島での実験に成功）。
	11月	アメリカ、エニウェトク環礁で初の水爆実験。
1953年	7月	朝鮮戦争休戦協定調印。
	8月	ソ連、水爆保有を発表。
1954年	3月	アメリカのビキニ環礁での水爆実験で、日本のマグロ漁船第五福竜丸被曝。
	5月	原水爆禁止署名運動、東京・杉並の主婦から全国に広がる。
1955年	3月	イギリス、水爆製造計画を発表。フランス、原爆製造計画を発表。
	8月	第1回原水爆禁止世界大会開催（以後、今日まで毎年開催される）。
1957年	5月	イギリス、クリスマス島で水爆実験。
	10月	ソ連、中国と国防新技術協定（原爆見本・製造資料の提供）を結ぶ。
	11月	日本原子力発電㈱設立。
1960年	2月	フランス、サハラ砂漠で初の原爆実験に成功。
	7月	アメリカ、原子力潜水艦からのポラリス核ミサイル水中発射に成功。
1961年	11月	国連総会、核兵器使用禁止宣言とアフリカ非核武装宣言を可決。
1962年	10月	アメリカ大統領ケネディ、ソ連がキューバにミサイル基地建設中と発表、キューバ海上封鎖を声明（キューバ危機）。
1963年	1月	アメリカ、原子力潜水艦の日本寄港を要求。
	8月	米英ソ、大気圏内・宇宙空間及び水中における核実験を禁止する条約（部分的核実験停止条約）に調印。
		フランス大統領ドゴール、同条約に不参加を表明。中国も反対を表明。
1964年	10月	中国、初の原爆実験に成功。
1968年	1月	日本政府、「非核三原則」を言明。
	7月	核不拡散条約（NPT）に62か国が調印。
1969年	9月	中国、水爆実験に成功。
1974年	5月	インド、核実験に成功。
1979年	3月	アメリカ、スリーマイル島原子力発電所で大量の放射能漏れ事故。
	12月	北大西洋条約機構（NATO）が、西欧5か国にアメリカ製の中距離核ミサイル配備を決定。
1981年	10月	アメリカ大統領レーガン、核戦力強化計画を発表。
		西ドイツのボンで30万人の反核集会。以後ヨーロッパ各地で大規模反核集会。
1982〜83年		反核運動、全世界的に盛り上がる。
1986年	4月	ソ連、チェルノブイリ原子力発電所で大事故。
1991年	1月	湾岸戦争始まる。アメリカ軍、劣化ウラン弾を使用。
1995年	1月	アメリカ・スミソニアン博物館で「原爆展」中止を決定。
	5月	核不拡散条約（NPT）を無期限延長。中国、地下核実験実施を発表。
	9月	フランス、ムルロワ環礁で地下核実験。
1996年	9月	国連総会、あらゆる核実験を禁止する包括的核実験禁止条約（CTBT）を採択。
1997年	3月	動燃核燃料再処理工場（JCO、茨城県東海村）で爆発・火災事故。
	7月	アメリカ、初の臨界前核実験を実施。
1998年	5月	インド、パキスタン両国が核実験（核兵器保有を言明）。
2001年	7月	アメリカ・ブッシュ政権、包括的核実験禁止条約（CTBT）に反対を表明、地下核実験再開の可能性を示唆。
2003年	1月	北朝鮮、核不拡散条約（NPT）脱退を宣言。
	3月	イラク戦争始まる。アメリカ軍、劣化ウラン弾を使用。
2004年		「核の闇市場」（核の拡散）が明るみに出る。
		2005年5月に国連で行なわれる核不拡散条約（NPT）再検討会議に向けての署名運動が世界的に開始される。

A Chronology of Atomic Weapons and Nuclear Power

October 1941	U.S. President Roosevelt orders the development of the atomic bomb.
June 1942	U.S. Army begins work on the Manhattan Project, the research leading to the invention of the atomic bomb.
16 July 1945	U.S. successfully tests the world's first atomic bomb in New Mexico, U.S.A. U.S.President Truman orders the deployment of the atomic bomb, Hiroshima , Kokura, Niigata, and Nagasaki are designated as possible targets.
6 August 1945	8:15 a.m. Atomic bomb (uranium) dropped on Hiroshima.
9 August 1945	11:02 a.m. Atomic bomb (plutonium) dropped on Nagasaki.
July 1946	United States tests a hydrogen bomb on the Bikini Atoll.
August 1949	Soviet Union conducts its first atomic bomb test.
January 1950	President Truman orders the production of hydrogen bombs.
June 1950	Start of the Korean War. In November Truman announces that use of nuclear weapons is under consideration.
September 1951	Signing of the San Francisco Peace Treat and the Japan-U.S. Security Treaty.
February 1952	Great Britain announces possession of an atomic bomb. In October it runs a successful test in the Monte Bello Islands in the South Pacific.
November 1952	United States runs its first test of a hydrogen bomb in the Enewetok Atoll.
July 1953	Signing of a ceasefire in the Korean War.
August 1953	The Soviet Union announces possession of a hydrogen bomb.
March 1954	United States tests a hydrogen bomb on the Bikini Atoll, exposing the Japanese tuna trawler "Lucky Dragon #5" to the radioactive fallout.
May 1954	A signature-collection campaign petitioning to abolish nuclear weapons begins in Suginami, Tokyo, and spreads throughout Japan.
March 1955	Great Britain announces its plans to produce a hydrogen bomb; France announces its plans to manufacture an atomic bomb.
August 1955	The first World Conference against Atomic and Hydrogen Bombs is held (It is held every year until today).
May 1957	Great Britain tests a hydrogen bomb on Christmas Island.
October 1957	Soviet Union and People's Republic of China sign an agreement to share national defense technologies (including prototypes of, and production information for, atomic bombs).
November 1957	Founding of the Japan Atomic Power Company.
February 1960	France tests a hydrogen bomb in the Sahara Desert
July 1960	United States successfully launches a Polaris missile, armed with a nuclear warhead, from a submerged, nuclear-powered submarine.
November 1961	The United Nations General Assembly passes a resolution banning the use of nuclear weapons and declaring the continent of Africa a nuclear weapons-free zone.
October 1962	U.S. President Kennedy exposes the Soviet construction of nuclear missile bases in Cuba, and calls for a blockade (the Cuban Missile Crisis).
January 1963	United States requests docking rights in Japan for its nuclear powered submarines.
August 1963	United States, Great Britain, and the Soviet Union sign the Treaty Banning Nuclear Weapon Tests in the Atmosphere, in Outer Space and Under Water (the Partial Test Ban Treaty). President de Gaulle announces France's non participation. The People's Republic of China also declares its opposition.
October 1964	China successfully completes its first nuclear test.
January 1968	The Japanese government declares its three anti-nuclear principles.
July 1968	Sixty-two nations sign the Treaty on the Non-Proliferation of Nuclear Weapons (NPT).
September 1969	China successfully completes a hydrogen bomb test.
May 1974	India successfully tests a nuclear weapon.
March 1979	A partial core meltdown at the Three Mile Island Nuclear Power Plant in the United States results in the emission of large amounts of radiation.
December 1979	The North Atlantic Treaty Organization (NATO) passes a resolution to deploy U.S.-made medium range missiles in five western European nations.
October 1981	U.S. President Reagan announces forthcoming improvements in the U.S. nuclear arsenal. An anti-nuclear demonstration in Bonn, West Germany, draws crowds numbering 300,000; massive protests follow in numerous European locations.
1982~83	The anti-nuclear movement sees rapid world-wide growth.
April 1986	Major accident at the Chernobyl Nuclear Power Plant in the Soviet Union.
January 1991	Start of the Gulf War ("Operation Desert Storm"). U.S. troops use low-grade uranium munitions.
January 1995	Smithsonian National Air and Space Museum abandons its original plans for an atomic bomb exhibit.
May 1995	China (PRC) announces underground nuclear testing. Nuclear Non-Proliferation Treaty (NPT) Review and Extension Conference (NPTREC) extends the treaty indefinitely.
September 1995	France tests a nuclear weapon on the Mururoa Atoll.
September 1996	The United Nations General Assembly adopts a Comprehensive Test Ban Treaty (CTBT).
March 1997	Fire and explosion at the Japan Conversion Operation (Tokai Uranium Processing Plant).
July 1997	The United States conducts a sub-critical nuclear weapons test.
May 1998	Both India and Pakistan conduct nuclear tests (and both announce possession of atomic bombs).
July 2001	The Bush Administration in the U.S. indicates its opposition to the Comprehensive Nuclear Test Ban Treaty (CTBT) and hints it may recommence underground nuclear testing.
January 2003	North Korea announces its withdrawal from the Nuclear Non-Proliferation Treaty (NPT).
March 2003	United States and Great Britain invade Iraq, beginning the Iraq War. U.S. troops use low-grade uranium munitions.
2004	The existence of a "nuclear black market" contributing to the proliferation of nuclear weapons comes to light. In anticipation of a United Nations conference to re-examine the Nuclear Non-Proliferation Treaty (NPT) in May 2005 , a worldwide signature-collection campaign begins.

ヒロシマの鳩
山下蘇朴

「碧空の高きより飛べ白鳩の
平和の使者となりて世界へ──蘇朴」

Dove Over Hiroshima.
Yamashita Masato

"In skies of blue
The white dove
Soaring high
A messenger of peace
Speaking to all the world ─ by Masato"

武器　　　　山田かん

人間と人間と―
武器もつものと持たないものと
人間が人間を―
武器もつ腕が拳の腕を
人間は人間を―
bombもつものは持たないものを
人間に人間が―
胸板に銃口を擬し
人間は人間に―
武器もつものは持たないものに
破れさった生活とたたかいが
仲間から仲間へ―
黒い鴉と灰色の鴉にわれわれは
仲間から仲間へ―
殺されるものと殺すものと
叫びから叫びへ―
武器なきものは武器持つものを

Weapons　　　**Yamada Kan**

One human and another
One with weapons and one without
One human to another
The hand with a weapon to the hand clenched in a fist
One human to another
One with the bomb to one without
One human has another
Jam the muzzle of a rifle to his chest
One human to another
One with weapons to the one without
Shattered lives and warring
Passed from friend to friend
We are controlled by ravens of black and ravens of grey
Passed from friend to friend
Those killed and those killing
From cry to cry
Those without weapons to those fully armed

やまだ・かん（1930〜2003）長崎県生まれ。詩人。爆心地より2.7kmの地で被爆。長崎における詩作活動の中心人物として活躍。詩集に『記憶の固執・山田かん詩集エッセイ集』『ナガサキ・腐蝕する暦日の底で』などがある。

Yamada Kan (1930~2003) was born in Nagasaki; he was 2.7 kilometers from ground zero when the bomb was dropped. A poet, Yamada was a key player in those circles in Nagasaki. His published work includes Kioku no koshitsu (The persistence of memory) and Nagasaki: fushoku suru rekijitsu no soko de (Nagasaki: The depths of a corrupted calendar).

あとがき

なぜ人類は「核」を生み出してしまったのだろう。科学の発達による必然的結果であるとはいえ、「ヒロシマ・ナガサキ」の出来事を考え、またその後も開発が続けられた「核」の在り方を思うと、原始主義だといわれようが、「核＝原水爆・原発」の存在しない世界を想定しないわけにはいかない。

たった1発の爆弾で30万人以上が暮らす一つの都市が壊滅し、そこで生活していた人間の大半を殺された事実、そして生き残った人びとも「被爆者」として生きながらの死を生きなければならない現実は、「核」という存在が非人間的なものの極致にあること、またこの地球と人類の「未来」を阻むものであることを証している。

作家の大江健三郎が若き日に広島を訪れ、原爆病で苦しむ被爆者と彼らの治療に取り組む原爆病院の医師に出会って、「自分自身の感覚とモラルと思想とを、すべて単一の広島のヤスリにかけ、広島のレンズをとおして再検討することを望んだ」（『ヒロシマ・ノート』1965年）と決意したことの意味を、「ヒロシマ・ナガサキ」から60年経った今、改めて私たちは考えなければならないのではないか。それは、「未来」を次の世代にわたすべく現在を生きる私たちの責務である。

本書を世に送る意味もそこにある。日本のみならず全世界の、現代が「平和」であると思っている人も、またイラクのように戦火の下にある人も、核状況の原点である「ヒロシマ・ナガサキ」の出来事を知ってほしいのである。そして、「核」の非人間性（反地球的存在）とそれがもたらす「悲劇」について真摯に考えてほしいのである。「核」は、人間が生み出した悪魔のような存在である。「核」による人間の支配を許してはならない。本書の編集にあたって、切にそう思う。

清水博義
黒古一夫

Afterword

Why did humankind tap the power of the atom? On one hand, it may very well have been the inevitable next step in scientific development. Nevertheless, on the other hand, the fact that some have continued to explore nuclear potentials even after the tragedies of Hiroshima and Nagasaki is surely reason enough for us to consider taking what might seem like a step backward, a return to a world free from nuclear weapons and power plants.

The detonation of a single bomb destroyed an entire city. Half of its population of over 300,000 died as a result, and the radiation exposure condemned the survivors to lives lived with death never more than a half-step behind them. Surely this alone is overwhelming evidence that the unleashing of nuclear energy is both inhuman in the extreme and poses a grave threat to the future of humankind and the earth.

In his *Hiroshima Notes* (1965), writer Oe Kenzaburo describes how as a young man he visited Hiroshima and met with both victims suffering from radiation sickness and the doctors who struggled to treat them in hospitals dedicated to that purpose. "Thereafter my aspiration has been to hone my personal sensitivities, my morals, and my philosophy against the whetstone of that singular event which is Hiroshima, and to re-think them all through that lens," he wrote. Today, sixty years after the events at Hiroshima and Nagasaki, we must again ponder the significance of that commitment. Such is our duty as humans alive today and preparing to hand over the future to the next generation.

These beliefs are our motivation for presenting this collection of photographs and images to world. The events of Hiroshima and Nagasaki are the origin of all things nuclear, and we want what transpired there to be known the world over—by those in Japan and throughout the world who believe this is a time of peace, by those who, like the people of Iraq, now live in the shadow of war. It is our wish that people reflect sincerely on the inhuman nature of things nuclear, on the danger they pose to the earth, and on the tragedies they bring. Humans have unleashed the supernatural powers of a nuclear reaction; we must not allow them to control us. This fact has never been clearer to us than in the process of assembling the materials for this book.

Shimizu Hiroyoshi
Kuroko Kazuo

●参考文献

『長崎 よみがえる原爆写真』NHK取材班　NHK出版　1995年

『図録 ヒロシマを世界に』広島平和記念資料館編・刊　1999年

「アサヒグラフ」（1952年8月6日号）朝日新聞社

『広島——戦争と都市』（岩波写真文庫72）岩波書店編集部編　岩波書店　1952年

『原爆第一号ヒロシマの写真記録』梅野彪・田島賢裕編　朝日出版社　1952年

『写真でみる原爆の記録』原水爆資料保存会　1958年

『写真集 原爆をみつめる——1945年 広島・長崎』飯島宗一・相原秀次編　岩波書店　1981年

『記録写真 原爆の長崎』北島宗人編　第一出版社　1952年

『写真記録 ヒロシマ25年』佐々木雄一郎　朝日新聞社　1970年

『ヒロシマは生きていた——佐々木雄一郎の記録』佐々木雄一郎写真　毎日新聞社広島支局編・刊　1977年

『ヒロシマ』土門拳　研光社　1958年

『写真記録 原爆棄民 ——韓国・朝鮮人被爆者の証言』伊藤孝司　ほるぷ出版　1987年

『広島壊滅のとき——被爆カメラマン写真集』広島原爆被災撮影者の会編・刊　1981年

『母と子でみる 原爆を撮った男たち』反核・写真運動編　草の根出版会　1987年

『ヒロシマ』土田ヒロミ　佼正出版社　1985年

『ヒロシマ ナガサキ 原爆写真・絵画集成』（全6巻）家永三郎ほか編　日本図書センター　1993年

『日本の原爆記録』（全20巻）家永三郎ほか編　日本図書センター　1991年

●協力

広島平和記念資料館　長崎原爆資料館　日本リアリズム写真集団広島支部

日本リアリズム写真集団長崎支部　原爆の図丸木美術館　広島県立美術館

広島市現代美術館　平和博物館を創る会　朝日新聞社　毎日新聞社　中国新聞社

機関紙連合通信社　長崎平和研究所　伊藤眞理子

＊本書の収録作品のなかに、写真撮影者など不明のものがあります。お気付きの方は、日本図書センターまでご連絡下さいますようお願いいたします。

＊本文中の写真や絵画などの説明文は、関連の文献や撮影者の談話などに基づいて執筆しています。また、絵画作品中の文字を書き起こしたものは、誤字を正し現代的な表記に改めた箇所があります。

●編者紹介

黒古一夫 1945年生まれ。群馬県出身。文芸評論家・筑波大学教授。著書に『北村透谷論』（冬樹社）、『大江健三郎論―森の思想と生き方の原理』（彩流社）、『野間宏―人と文学』（勉誠出版）など多数。原爆関係の著書に『原爆とことば―原民喜から林京子まで』（三一書房）、『原爆文学論―核時代と想像力』（彩流社）、編著に『日本の原爆文学』（全15巻・ほるぷ出版）、『日本の原爆記録』（全20巻・日本図書センター）、『ヒロシマ ナガサキ原爆写真・絵画集成』（全6巻・日本図書センター）。監修に『原爆文献大事典』（日本図書センター）などがある。

清水博義 1933年生まれ。大阪府出身。ほるぷ出版取締役編集担当・代表取締役を経て、フリー編集者・ライター。編書に『日本の原爆文学』（全15巻・ほるぷ出版）、『日本の原爆記録』（全20巻・日本図書センター）、『ヒロシマ ナガサキ原爆写真・絵画集成』（全6巻・日本図書センター）、『写真記録・アメリカの歴史』（全4巻・ほるぷ出版）など多数。著書に『結城座への招待状』（ネット武蔵野）など。

●翻訳者紹介

James Dorsey（ジェイムス・ドーシー）1961年生まれ。ニューヨーク出身。ワシントン大学アジア言語文学部大学院でPh. D（日本文学）を修得。現在ダートマス大学アジア・中近東言語文学部助教授。主に小林秀雄、坂口安吾を中心に〈戦争と文学者の関係〉を研究。法政大学に2年、筑波大学に1年留学。論文に「小林秀雄論」、「坂口安吾論」などがある。

●Edit

Kuroko Kazuo, born in 1945, is a literary critic and professor at Tsukuba University. His many published works include a study of Nobel laureate Oe Kenzaburo as well as research on atomic bomb literature. In the capacity of editor, Kuroko has also participated in the compilation of collected works and anthologies treating documents, literary works, photographs, and art connected to the atomic bombs.

Shimizu Hiroyoshi, a freelance writer and editor, was born in 1933. He has edited picture books as well as historical and literary works; teaming up with Kuroko, he has also compiled numerous volumes related to the atomic bombings.

●Translate

James Dorsey was born in New York in 1961. He earned a Ph.D. in Japanese literature from the Department of Asian Languages and Literatures at the University of Washington, and now works as an associate professor of Japanese in the Department of Asian and Middle Eastern Languages and Literatures at Dartmouth College. His research focuses on the relationship of literary figures to the war, and he has published studies of the critic Kobayashi Hideo and the writer Sakaguchi Ango.

原爆写真　ノーモア　ヒロシマ・ナガサキ
No More Hiroshima, Nagasaki

初版第1刷発行　2005年3月25日

［編　者］	黒古一夫　清水博義
［翻訳者］	James Dorsey
［発行者］	高野義夫
［発行所］	株式会社　日本図書センター
	東京都文京区大塚3-8-2
	TEL.03-3947-9387（営業部）／TEL.03-3945-6448（出版部）
	http://www.nihontosho.co.jp
［印刷・製本］	図書印刷　株式会社
［装幀・アートディレクション］	小林健三
［レイアウト］	有限会社　ニコリデザイン
［編集スタッフ］	佐藤祐子　関澤裕子　大西夏奈子

ISBN4-8205-1940-9　C0070

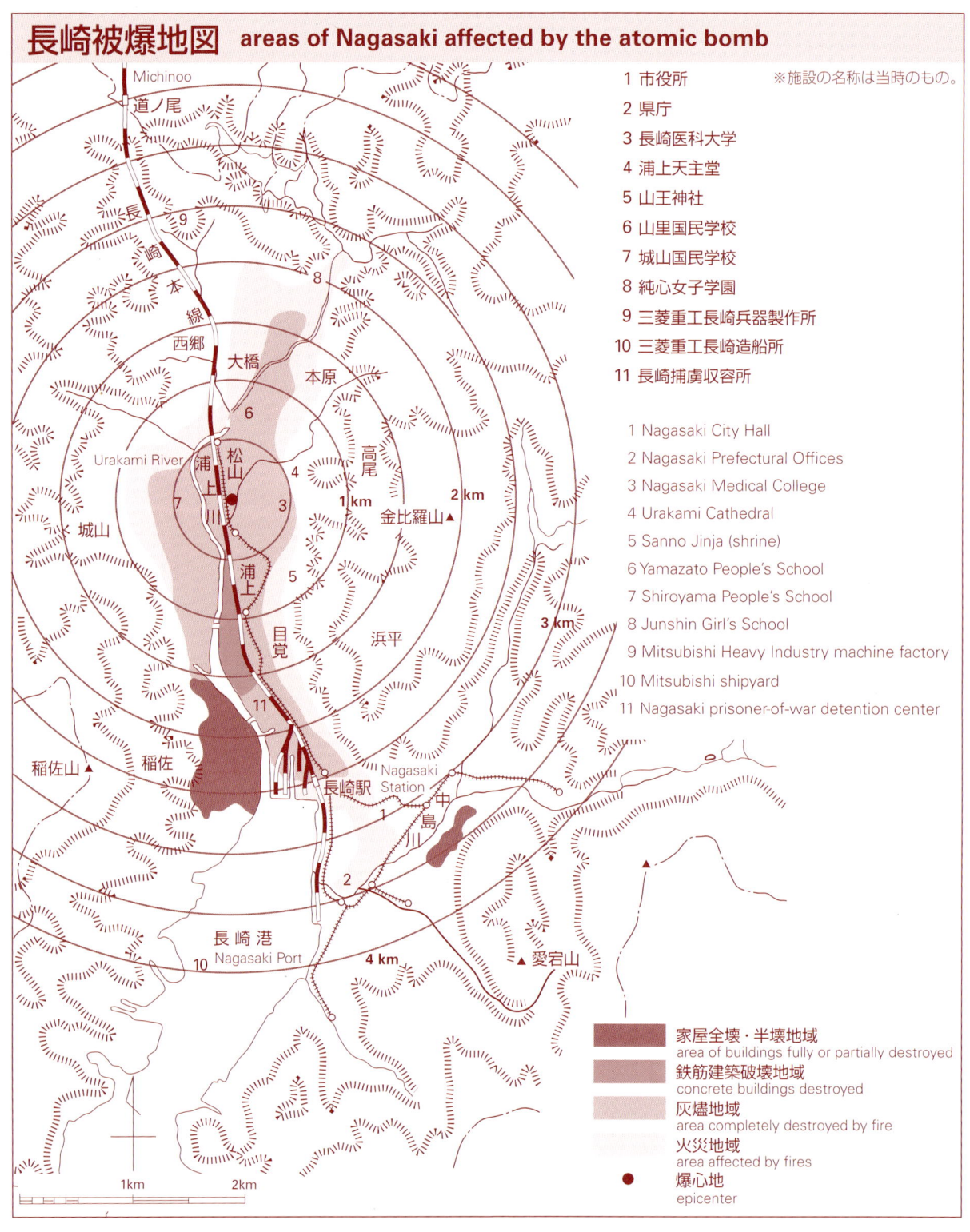

長崎被爆地図　areas of Nagasaki affected by the atomic bomb

※施設の名称は当時のもの。

1 市役所
2 県庁
3 長崎医科大学
4 浦上天主堂
5 山王神社
6 山里国民学校
7 城山国民学校
8 純心女子学園
9 三菱重工長崎兵器製作所
10 三菱重工長崎造船所
11 長崎捕虜収容所

1 Nagasaki City Hall
2 Nagasaki Prefectural Offices
3 Nagasaki Medical College
4 Urakami Cathedral
5 Sanno Jinja (shrine)
6 Yamazato People's School
7 Shiroyama People's School
8 Junshin Girl's School
9 Mitsubishi Heavy Industry machine factory
10 Mitsubishi shipyard
11 Nagasaki prisoner-of-war detention center

Michinoo
道ノ尾
長崎本線
西郷
大橋
本原
高尾
Urakami River
浦上川
松山
浦上天主堂
城山
金比羅山▲
浦上
目覚
浜平
1km　2km　3km
稲佐山▲　稲佐
長崎駅　Nagasaki Station
中島川
長崎港 Nagasaki Port
4 km
▲愛宕山

家屋全壊・半壊地域
area of buildings fully or partially destroyed

鉄筋建築破壊地域
concrete buildings destroyed

灰燼地域
area completely destroyed by fire

火災地域
area affected by fires

● 爆心地
epicenter

1km　2km